£8.00

The Book of Canoeing

Dennis J. Davis

The Book of Canoeing

ARTHUR BARKER LIMITED
5 Winsley Street London W1

To Katherine and Patrick

© 1969 by Dennis J. Davis

SBN 213 17804 4

Phototypeset by BAS Printers Limited, Wallop, Hampshire
and printed by Unwin Brothers Limited, Woking

Contents

Illustrations

Photographs

Drawings

Introduction

Canoeing is a many sided sport; you can paddle a canoe in little more than a ditch or across the Channel, down the rapids of a Welsh river or the quiet of an English trout stream. If you want competition you can sprint at international level or in a club regatta, enter the rough water obstacle race that is canoe slalom or paddle down a disused canal in a long distance race. All these are canoeing, all these could be canoeing to you.

There is only one important proviso – you *must* be able to swim. Really swim, not just dog-paddle across an indoor pool. Fifty yards is a reasonable minimum distance. This requirement is not because as a canoeist you will necessarily indulge in very much swimming but as a means of ensuring your own safety in an emergency.

Because canoeing has so many varied aspects it is impossible to deal with them all in a one-volume book, indeed, some aspects cannot be adequately covered in a book at all and need practical demonstration for their proper explanation. For this reason I have considered canoeing as a recreation rather than a sport; far more canoeists use their canoes for touring and day trips than ever enter a competitive event. It is my intention that the beginner should be able to pick up this book, learn a little of the history of canoeing, how to build his (or her) canoe, how to use it and how to maintain it in good condition.

Somewhere early in his canoeing life, the beginner should consider joining a club. If you do not know the address of your nearest canoe club the General Secretary of the British Canoe Union (BCU) will be able to advise you. The BCU is the body which controls canoeing in this country and is affiliated to the International Canoe Federation. More details on the BCU are given in the last chapter.

Canoeing does not have to be an expensive pastime; at present-day prices you will be able to make your canoe, make or buy a paddle and other accessories for less than £20.

The information on competitive canoeing has been obtained with a view to ensuring that it is as up to date as possible; rules and regulations do change however and where appropriate further information should be sought at the time it is required.

I should like to thank those people who gave information; Black and Edgington Ltd, who supplied the Good Companions Minor tent; and lastly, but most important, my model.

1 A brief history of canoeing

Canoeing is a relatively young sport, being little more than one hundred years old. However, craft which might be described as the forerunners of the modern canoe have been in use for many hundreds of years. Perhaps the oldest of these is the dug-out canoe made from a single tree trunk, hollowed and with the outside roughly shaped. For this craft to work at all the tree from which it is made must be very large. This has confined the use of the dug-out canoe to those countries, mainly in the tropics, where sufficiently large trees are freely available. In parts of tropical Africa the dug-out may still be seen in use.

Far more sophisticated in design and construction are the sea going types of Eskimo kayak and the American Indian birch bark canoe. These two types of canoe are of very different design but both fulfil their intended purpose admirably.

The Eskimo kayak, used for seal hunting in the icy seas off Greenland, is designed to carry the hunter and his equipment only. The paddler seals himself into the kayak by fastening the bottom of his anorak over the rim of the small circular cockpit. This permits self rescue in the event of a capsize by means of the Eskimo roll; failing this the Eskimo would die in a few minutes in the freezing water.

The kayak is made from a framework of wood covered with sealskins carefully sewn together. The stitches are made without penetrating the thickness of the skin to minimise the possibility of leaks.

The paddler sits low in the kayak with his legs outstretched before him and uses a double-bladed paddle dipped into the water on each side of the kayak. The kayak has to be quite narrow if a long, unwieldy paddle is to be avoided. A

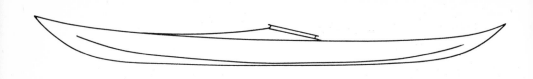

Figure 1 Eskimo Kayak.

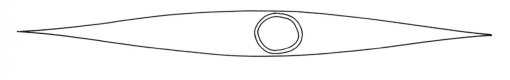

typical Greenland kayak might be 19 feet long with a beam of about 19 inches. These dimensions provide an excellent sea canoe for the expert and several modern versions are available with either a wooden frame, canvas covered or made completely from thin waterproof plywood. Both types retain the hard chine shape and slender lines of the original.

The American Indian birch bark canoe is a very different craft. The Indian made his canoe as the only alternative to walking as a means of travel in the forests where he lived. It was designed therefore as a load carrier suitable for use both on the wild rivers and lakes of North America. As the canoe was built in forest lands it was made entirely of wood. The outer skin was of birch bark which gives the canoe its name. This was cut and curved to the required shape, preferably from a single piece of bark, then sewn with supple roots to a horizontal frame made up of gunwale strips and thwarts. Into the resulting shell were bent thin cedar ribs which were jammed under the gunwale strips. Finally the hull was completed by forcing thin planking between the ribs and the outer skin of birch bark. Any seams or stitching were then sealed with natural gum.

To facilitate its role as a load carrier the Indian canoe is open except for a small strengthening deck at each end. It is made deeper and broader than the Eskimo kayak to enable it to ride over rapids or waves rather than through them. The original birch bark varied enormously in size depending upon

12

its purpose – some war canoes are reputed to have been 30 feet long – but typical modern dimensions for this type of canoe are 14 to 17 feet long with a beam of $2\frac{1}{2}$ to 3 feet.

The Indian used a single bladed paddle on one side of the canoe only and to achieve maximum efficiency he chose to kneel close to the side on which he was paddling. This enabled him to keep his paddle almost vertical and gave a high, powerful position well suited to the single bladed paddle and the beamy birch bark canoe.

The Indian canoe was quickly adopted by the white man who then evolved his own methods of construction while retaining the original shape. Two main forms of construction came into use; the American, which produced the 'canvas covered canoe', made with wide ribs, planked with thin boards and then covered with painted canvas to make it waterproof – a modern version of the birch bark, in fact. The Canadian form is of all wood construction with the planks carefully butted together along their length to provide a watertight skin. The planks butt together so closely that no other sealing is necessary. The ribs used for this construction are narrow and closely spaced. Many canoes of this type have been imported into England and the majority of the open

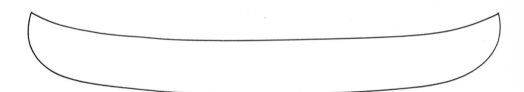

Figure 2 Canadian canoe.

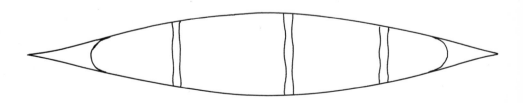

canoes built here have been of this construction.

The all wood canoe is rather more liable to suffer damage than the 'canvas covered' variety and is in this respect less suited to rapid river work. More recently Canadian canoes, as the open type are called in this country, have been made from moulded plywood or glass-fibre reinforced plastics.

Canoeing as a pastime really began about the middle of the nineteenth century when decked canoes started to make their appearance on the Thames. These were based on the Eskimo kayak but bore little resemblance to it, being shorter and much broader, about 15 by $2\frac{1}{2}$ feet. A double paddle was used for propulsion but the canoeists lacked the skill of the Eskimo. In 1865 John MacGregor put canoeing on the map by writing his *One Thousand Miles in the Rob Roy Canoe,* an account of his voyage through Europe in an all wood, decked canoe. This book is a canoeing classic and well worth reading if you can find a copy. A year later MacGregor and some friends formed the Canoe Club which in 1873 became the Royal Canoe Club, still very much in being today at Teddington on the Thames. The Club organised races but also began to sail the canoes, an action which led to the decline of canoeing for the already heavy wooden canoe became a proper sailing craft and evolved into the present-day 10 square metre sailing canoe which is probably the fastest single-handed sailing monohull available – but not much like the canoes we are concerned with!

Canoeing received a boost in the early 1900s when a German, Hans Klepper, invented the folding canoe. By the 1930s the folding canoe, already a hit with young people in Germany, began to make its appearance in this country and later in the decade was beginning to be made here.

In 1936 the British Canoe Union came into being and a British canoe team was sent to Germany for the Olympic Games of that year. Folding canoes became the most popular type but were quite expensive. Less convenient but far cheaper was the lath and canvas rigid canoe. This consists of a wooden framework, rather like a model aircraft frame, which is then covered with canvas or a canvas/

plastic material. These are fairly easy to build and many different designs are available. Some disadvantages are the difficulty of getting the skin sufficiently tight and the fact that the hull shape is a series of flats where the canvas stretches across the stringers.

At this stage the Second World War started and private canoeing again faded into the background; however, canoes of various types were used during the war – some were even transported to the enemy coast in the torpedo tubes of submarines! Wartime research also produced better quality waterproof glues and made possible reliable waterproof plywood. This in turn led to the development of canoes made from thin veneers of wood moulded and glued together under pressure. Canoes of this form were found to be light and strong but rather expensive because of the costly equipment required to produce them. Today almost the only canoes made using this method are those used for racing. These are beautifully made but are hardly practical for normal canoeing.

After the 1939–45 war canoeing began again to climb into popularity with the folding canoe as the mainstay of the sport. The rigid framed canoe retained its hold, too, on the less wealthy canoeists and many improved designs were produced. The sporting or competitive aspects of canoeing began to grow and slalom, which had started during the 1930s and takes its name from the similar sport in skiing, was beginning to be taken seriously. The canoe slalom course is arranged in rough water, often below a weir on an otherwise staid river such as the Thames. Pairs of poles are suspended over the water to form gates, the poles are striped red and white or green and white to indicate the entry side, i.e. red is left to port. The gates are numbered and carefully arranged in order to make the canoeist use all his skill in covering the course. Each run is timed and penalties awarded for infringements such as touching a gate or passing through one in the wrong direction. Further complications may be introduced by the organisers of the slalom.

Canoe sprint racing has always been part of the sport but it was only in the 1940s with the advent of the moulded

veneer canoe that paddling standards really began to improve. Modern sprint racing is very much an international affair with a win at the Olympic Games as the goal. The distances do not sound like sprints – 500, 1,000 and 10,000 metres!

Long distance racing is one of the most popular forms of canoe sport because it is the one aspect where a very specialised type of canoe is not essential. The best known long distance race is also the longest in Britain, from Devizes in Wiltshire to Westminster Bridge, a distance of 125 miles along canal, river and tideway.

During the post-war period of social change even canoeing could not be overlooked. With the growth in ownership of motor cars the popularity of the folding canoe began to decline – it is as easy to carry one or two rigid canoes on a roof rack as a folding canoe in the boot of a car. Canoe makers experimented with new materials for rigid canoes and designs were produced for hard chine canoes using marine grade plywood. These were of conventional boat construction which involves making a frame which is in turn clad with thin plywood. Some of the more popular of this type were built to designs conforming with National Chine Kayak rules, newly introduced by the BCU to encourage the production of inexpensive racing canoes.

Canoe manufacturers were quick to see the possibilities of glass-fibre reinforced plastics and this construction is now supreme for slalom and rough water canoeing. It is not a suitable method of construction for the amateur unless he is prepared to go to a lot of trouble learning the technique of moulding. The amount of work involved in making the mould is such that it is just not worthwhile for only one boat.

Another method of producing hard chine canoes was devised by Mr K. Littledyke. This avoided the use of a framework by stitching pre-cut panels of plywood together with copper wire and reinforcing the joint with glass-fibre tape and resin. A few designs have also been produced using this method with more than two panels on each side. This

Plate 1 (*opposite*) A glass-fibre canoe being used for Eskimo rolling.

17

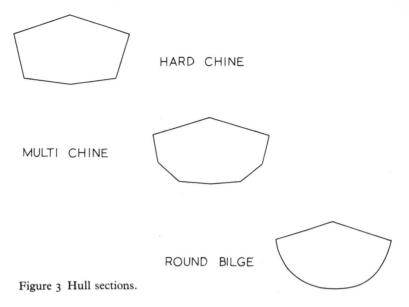

HARD CHINE

MULTI CHINE

ROUND BILGE

Figure 3 Hull sections.

gives an approximation to a round bilge hull but involves additional jointing.

The round bilge hull has a number of advantages; generally it is faster – given canoes of similar dimensions – and when building with thin plywood curved panels are more resistant to impact damage than flat. Until recently it was necessary to build a mould or jig in order to produce a round bilge hull from plywood but the DK designs have altered this situation. Canoes to these designs are built using a method I have devised which enables a round bilge hull to be made without the need for moulds, jigs or building boards. Indeed, only for one short stage does any of the canoe have to be fastened down; for the remainder of the building period it may be moved or even hung from the roof between building sessions. It is, therefore, an ideal method for schools, groups or individuals who are building in a space which must be utilised for other purposes.

While it is possible to build a *DK* canoe single handed it is also quite feasible for a number of people to be working on the separate parts since, apart from the deck, these may all be prepared before construction begins. This is particularly

18

useful for schools as in this way several pupils can play a part in building the canoe.

In the next chapter I will describe in detail how to build a *DK 12* single seat canoe using this method. Do read through the whole of the chapter and study the drawings and photographs before you begin to build your canoe.

2 Building a single seat canoe

In this chapter you will find full details on how to build a *DK 12* single seat canoe suitable for touring and the occasional long distance race. Make absolutely sure you understand each stage before actually trying to carry it out. You will find some stages easier if you can persuade a friend to assist. Help is particularly useful when fitting the keelson and again for marking out and fitting the decks. At the end of the chapter you will find a list of the tools you will need and a materials list.

The first thing to do is to decide which is the best side of the sheet of plywood you are going to use for the hull. Put the other sheet away as it will not be required until the hull is completed – if you can find space for it to lean against the wall in a garage or shed it will not come to any harm.

Mark a centre line on the best side of the hull plywood. It is advisable to do the marking out on the best side so that any tearing from the saw will be on the inside, although if a fine toothed panel or tenon saw is used there will be very little roughness. Continue to mark out this sheet as shown on the drawing. Letter and number the ends lightly with a soft pencil before cutting out as this will help identify the panels for fitting together. Cut out the four panels allowing a little waste outside the line. After cutting out plane the panels so the two sides of the canoe are exactly the same shape and size. The ends to be joined must be square and have right-angled corners to enable the joint to be checked for squareness when it is being glued.

At the bow and stern ends of the panels drill the holes which will be used when the ends are fastened together with short lengths of copper wire. These holes are $\frac{1}{4}$ inch from the keel edge of the panel and at $2\frac{1}{2}$-inch centres, i.e. $2\frac{1}{2}$ inches

Figure 4 (*opposite*) Hull ply layout.

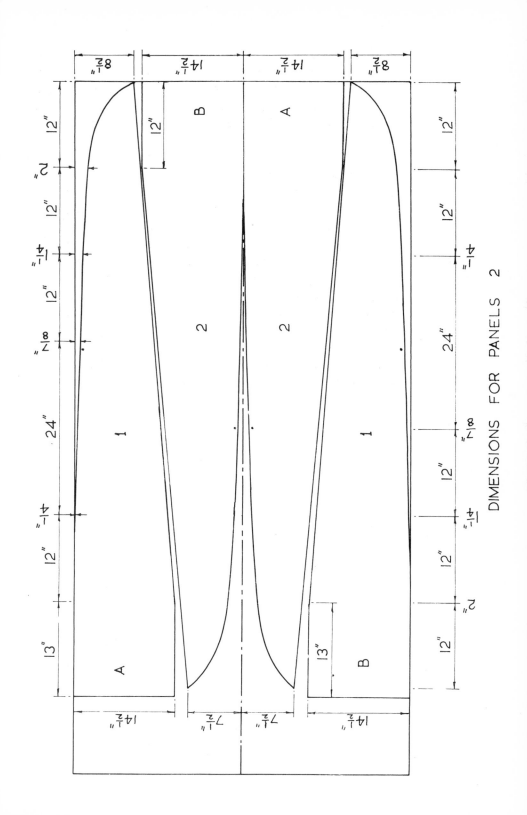

DIMENSIONS FOR PANELS 2

apart. It is not necessary to buy a drill for this job; the holes may be drilled quite satisfactorily by using a panel pin with its head snipped off or even with a small bradawl used carefully. Start making the holes about one inch down from the gunwale line and stop when you reach the approximate position shown on figure 4; it does not matter if you make a few too many as they will be covered by the keel.

The next stage is to join the two pairs of hull panels together to form the two sides. The joint used is a scarf joint to retain the same hull thickness throughout. To mark out the joint turn the four panels with *inside* of those number-ed one and the *outside* of those numbered two uppermost – the best side should be the outside. It is also convenient to have the square, numbered, ends of the panels together with the panels one on top of the other. Using a marking gauge set to one inch mark a line across the end of each of the four panels. If you do not have a marking gauge it is easy to make a simple one for this job with two pieces of wood and three nails as shown in figure 5. The marking gauge line must be made only on what is, for the moment, the top of each panel. You will see that when the panels are placed in their correct

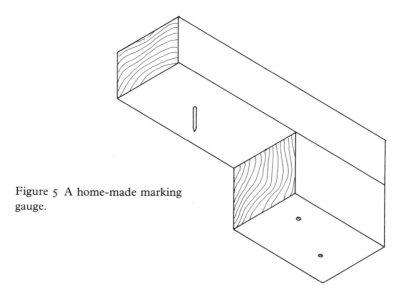

Figure 5 A home-made marking gauge.

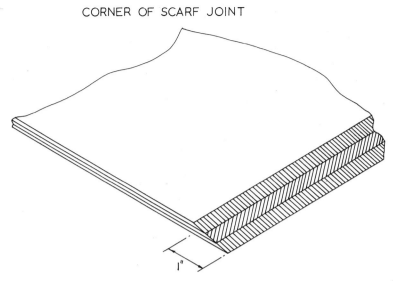

CORNER OF SCARF JOINT

Figure 6
Scarf joint.

1"

hull positions the gauge lines will come together and the stern panels will be overlapping those for the bow. Check that yours are correct before going on to the next stage.

For making the scarf joint you will need a sharp plane; one of the 'Surform' type will do but a really sharp smoothing plane is ideal. Cramp one of the hull panels to your bench or to a board so the end of the panel is fully supported and flush with the edge of the bench or board. If you have to use a board it should be a little longer than the width of the panels and at least 6 inches wide – a piece of $\frac{3}{4}$-inch thick blockboard is very suitable and can probably be bought cheaply as an offcut.

Plane the joint by planing between the gauge line and the *bottom* edge of the plywood. The planed surface must be flat and no thickness should be left at the end of the panel. If you find the bottom veneer of plywood tends to splinter angle the plane toward the edge. Once you have completed the first panel you will find the remaining three quite easy.

It is necessary now to prepare a piece of wood, 24 inches long by 2 inches wide by 1 inch thick, with one edge planed to a slightly convex curve. This will be cramped over the

23

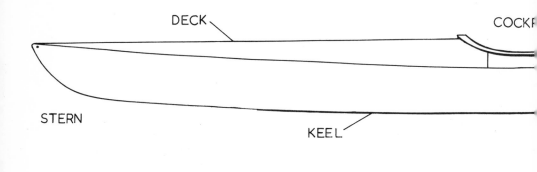

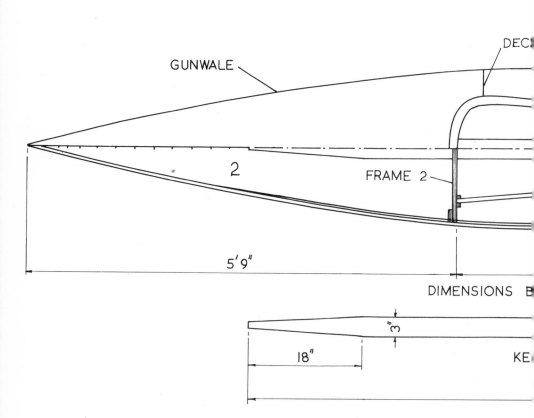

Figure 7 General arrangement drawing for the *DK12*.

24

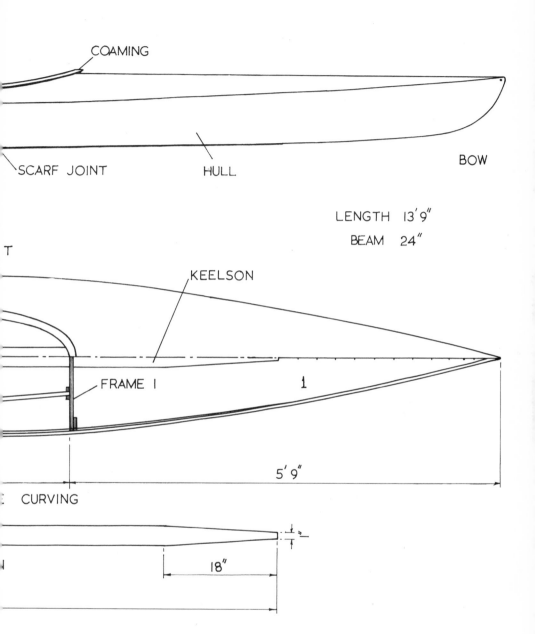

COAMING

SCARF JOINT   HULL   BOW

LENGTH 13' 9"
BEAM 24"

T

KEELSON

FRAME I   1

5' 9"

CURVING

18"

25

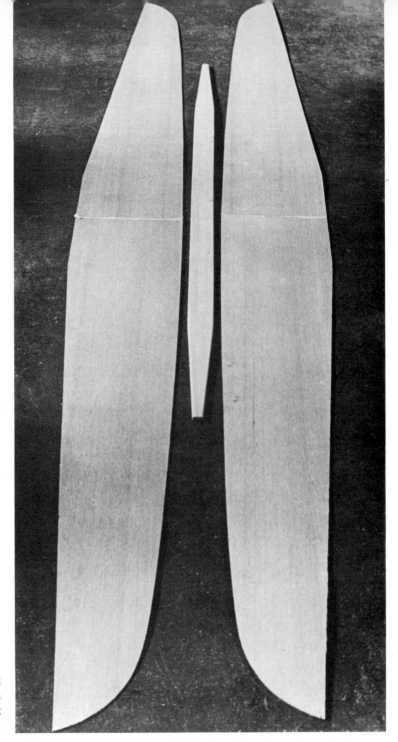

Plate 2 Hull panels and keelson ready for fixing together.

joint to ensure that the centre is held firmly while the glue is setting. Check that the curve is sufficient by cramping the wood to the bench or board, convex side down over a piece of newspaper. With the cramps at the ends of the wood it should be impossible to pull out the paper from the centre.

The glueing of the scarf joints is the one stage when the canoe must be left undisturbed until the glue has set; leaving it overnight is usually a convenient way of arranging this.

Place on your bench or board a sheet of newspaper; put on this the end of one of the panels with the planed part of the joint on top. Spread glue on the joint and place over it the appropriate panel. Check that the line of the scarf joint is at right angles to both the gunwale line and centre section of the keel line and pin both panels to the bench or board with two or three panel pins from which the heads have been snipped. Place another sheet of paper over the joint and cramp the piece of prepared wood over it, convex side down.

It is possible, with great care, to glue both scarf joints at the same time but it is safer to take a little longer and glue them separately. When glueing the second work over the first to ensure that both sides of the canoe finish the same size and shape.

When the glue has set remove the panels from the bench – do not forget to remove the headless panel pins! Scrape or glasspaper the glue and paper from the panels.

The keelson may be prepared while you are waiting for the scarf joint glue to set. Mark a centre line along the length of the underside of the keelson and plane it to shape as shown in figure 7. The top edges should be rounded slightly to improve its appearance. You are now ready to fix the hull panels to the keelson. Allow about two hours for this for, although it may not take so long, it is not a job which can be stopped before it is completed.

Spread glue on the underside of the keelson; if you are working in a warm atmosphere spread a foot or so at a time as the glue will begin to set before you are able to nail the panels down. Begin by fastening both panels to the keelson for a short distance each side of the scarf joint. Continue by nailing both panels up to the centre line of the keelson

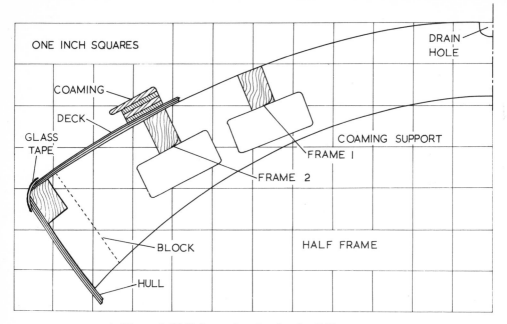

ONE INCH SQUARES

DRAIN HOLE

COAMING

DECK

GLASS TAPE

COAMING SUPPORT

FRAME I

FRAME 2

BLOCK

HALF FRAME

HULL

Figure 8 Half-frame drawing for the *DK12*.

working towards both ends of the hull in turn. The nails should be at about 2½-inch centres and staggered slightly to avoid the possibility of splitting the keelson. The whole procedure is eased if you can raise the section of the hull on which you are working by placing a small box or block under the keelson and allowing the rest of the hull to curve over the end of the bench. When the keelson is fitted the hull will be very curved along its length and rather saucer shaped. Leave the hull now until the glue is set. It may be moved but should have no further work carried out upon it at this stage.

The time taken for the glue to harden will not be wasted for you can be preparing the frames. Figure 8 must first be redrawn full size on to stiff paper marked out in 1-inch squares. To ensure maximum accuracy it is worth buying a sheet of paper already printed with the squares. Fold the paper vertically in half and draw the half frame as shown with its centre line at the fold. The paper frame may then be cut out and opened to the full size whole frame. Draw round this on to the ½-inch thick plywood to produce the two frames. Cut out the plywood frames using a coping or fret saw; leave them a little over length to allow for fitting to the hull and cut a fraction outside the line to allow for planing smooth with a 'Surform' plane or spokeshave.

Prepare the gunwale and coaming support blocks, nail and glue these to the frames in the positions shown. When the hull is ready pin and glue the gunwale strips into place. Use the $\frac{3}{4}$-inch brass pins at about 2-inch centres, pinning from the plywood into the gunwale strip. Start at the centre and work toward each end a short distance at a time. It is not necessary to work on both sides of the hull at the same time as it was when fixing the keelson. At the angle on the gunwale line allow the strip to take up a natural curve inside the angle until it is possible to fasten it flush with the edge of the panel again. The small overhanging piece of plywood will be planed off at a later stage. Allow the glue to set before continuing further.

Mark the frame positions on the gunwale strips. Note that the frame positions are shown measured to the *inner* side of the frames. Use sash cramps or a Spanish windlass to draw the sides of the hull together; position the cramps just inside the frame positions. As the gunwale strips approach the correct beam measurement place the frames in position and check their ends for fit. Adjust the ends as necessary and reduce the frames to the correct length; glue them into position and hold by tightening the cramps. Check they are parallel to each other. Do not remove the cramps or Spanish windlass.

Start to wire the ends of the hull together with the copper wire. Begin with the holes nearest to the end of the keelson and do not try to get the wires tight at first. If the wire is pulled gently as it is twisted it will be less liable to break. After three or four 'stitches' it will be possible to tighten earlier ones. Continue wiring to about 6 inches below the gunwale strips; as you near this point you will find it necessary to hold the gunwales together with a small cramp or a suitable steel screw which will be removed later. Cut the ends of the gunwale strips to the correct angle so they meet on the centre line when the hull plywood panels are just

Plate 3 Hull with
gunwale strips
fixed.

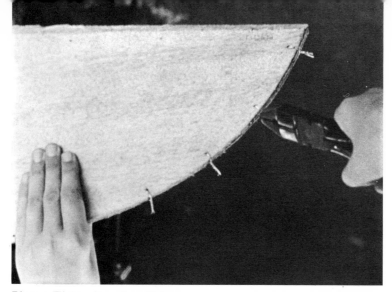

Plate 4 Tightening wire stitches.

touching. Glue the strips together where they meet and continue wiring up to the gunwale strips. This procedure is followed for both ends.

The most important detail of the wiring is to ensure that the hull panels come together without twisting. This will occur if one panel is allowed to slip below the other during the wiring process. Should this happen and be allowed to remain uncorrected the end of the canoe will have a twist which will adversely influence the handling of the completed craft.

When you are satisfied with the wiring the interior of the ends can be reinforced with glass-fibre tape and resin. For the remainder of the building instructions I shall refer to this process as 'taping'.

Mix the resin as necessary in accordance with the suppliers instructions. Two ounces should be sufficient for the interior of one end. Start by spreading a generous coat of the resin along the joint and about half an inch on each side of it. Tape this joint starting at the top, under the gunwale strips, pushing the tape well into the joint with a resin-loaded brush. Work along the joint in this way until the keelson is reached; tape over the end of this and cut the tape.

The tape must be kept flat against the hull plywood as far as possible and the resin worked well in with a stippling action. When the tape is properly impregnated it becomes clear. Any air bubbles must be worked out as they appear, or they will be a source of weakness. Treat both ends in this way and leave until dry.

The whole process is then repeated so there are two layers of tape in each end of the hull. It is preferable to leave the hull overnight to allow the resin to cure. Taping must not be attempted in a temperature of less than 60°F as the resin may not cure below this temperature. Any type of clean brush may be used to apply the resin; one about an inch wide will prove quite suitable.

The cramps or Spanish windlass may now be removed from the frames if the glue has had sufficiently long to set. Cut off the copper wire on the outside of the ends; this is easily done with pliers or pincers. Do not pull the wire through as in doing so you may disturb the inside taping. Clean off the outside of the ends with a 'Surform' plane or file. Where the keelson ends the hull plywood will tend to bend down a little; most of this plywood may be removed within the 1-inch width which will be covered by the tape. The edges of the plywood should be covered by the tape. The top of the ends may be rounded a little at this stage as shown on the profile drawing. Shaping the ends in this way is purely for appearance and is not essential.

The ends of the keel strip must then be shaped on the upper surface to fit the hull. When the shaping is completed the keel and ends will present a smooth, continuous line when viewed from the side. Pin and glue the keel strip into position.

Tape the outside of the ends following the instructions already given for taping the interior. If your canoe is likely to be used in shallow or rocky streams it is worthwhile protecting the whole keel by taping the full length of the boat. When the resin has cured, glasspaper it smooth and apply another coat of resin without tape. A good smooth finish will then be obtained after further glasspapering.

Cut the coaming supports to fit and glue them into place. The interior of the hull is now ready for varnishing. The use of varnish as a protective finish for small craft is something

Plate 5 Fitting keel.

of a tradition and for maximum protection it is a good idea to use one of the polyurethane variety. Follow the maker's instructions and do make sure the varnish you use is marine quality; ordinary varnish is quite useless for boats. Before you actually start to varnish, glasspaper inside the hull and remove any pencil marks – especially where they will be seen in the cockpit area. Give at least two coats of varnish taking care to get well into the ends which is where rot usually starts in wooden canoes. If you are using a conventional varnish thin the first coat with white spirit to ensure good penetration and give two further coats. Do not varnish the tops of the frames, gunwale strips or coaming supports. When the varnish is dry fair off the tops of the frames and gunwale strips. Quite a lot of planing will be necessary at the bow and stern to enable the deck plywood to lie flat at these points. Check the fit by holding the second sheet of plywood over the hull and pressing down to the gunwales.

Fit the deck by placing the plywood over the forward half of the hull, best side down, with one end just over-lapping the stem and one side overhanging the gunwale by about an inch at the point of maximum beam. Pin the sheet into position temporarily and pencil around the gunwale line leaving a little spare to allow for fitting when the deck

33

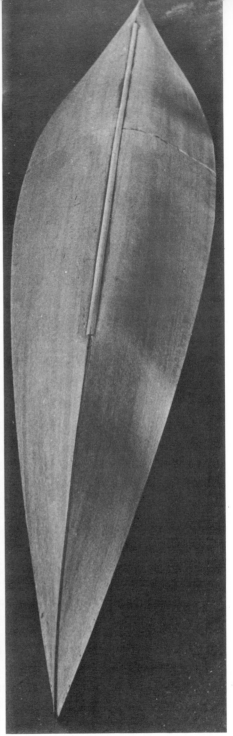

Plate 6 (*above*) Keel fixed.

Plate 7 (*left*) Interior ready for varnishing.

plywood is turned best side up. Pencil inside the coaming supports and frame one. Remove the sheet and cut out the foredeck; mark out the shape of the forward part of the cockpit from the details given in figure 9 and cut out the waste. Glasspaper and varnish the underside of the deck leaving clear those parts which will be glued when it is fixed. In fact you need varnish only that part forward of the frame because the side decks can be reached from in the cockpit after fixing.

The foredeck may then be glued and nailed into place using boat nails at about $2\frac{1}{2}$-inch centres. Centre the deck on the hull with nails at the stem and frame then commence nailing down at the frame – do not glue or nail the last two inches of side deck by the cockpit.

Mark out the stern deck in the same way but allow a 1-inch overlap where the two deck panels meet at the sides of the cockpit. Varnish and fix in the same way as the foredeck. At the overlap saw through both pieces of plywood with a tenon saw held at an angle of about 45 degrees *toward the bows*. Make lapping pieces from offcuts of plywood and glue them under the joints.

Plane off the waste at the gunwale and round off as shown. Tape the gunwale with one layer of tape and two of resin as

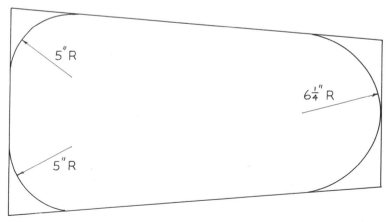

Figure 9 The cockpit shape.

5" R

6$\frac{1}{4}$" R

5" R

MAKE CARD TEMPLATES OF CORNERS

35

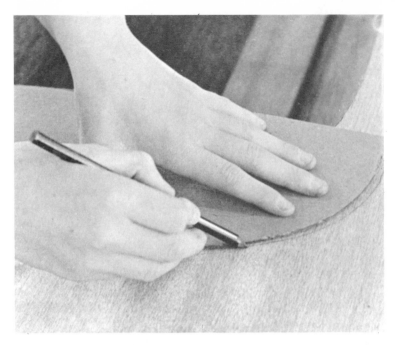

Plate 8 Marking out the cockpit shape.

described for the outside of the ends. When the resin is cured plane the deck to the cockpit line and fix the coaming which is made from offcuts of the 3-mm plywood. The outside of each piece must be finished before fixing while the inside can be spokeshaved smooth afterwards. Where the first layer of plywood has to be pinned through the deck only do not forget to snip off the ends of the pins and file off any remaining roughness.

Painter holes may be drilled through the hull at the ends just below the deck to ensure that the drill passes through the gunwale strips. A $\frac{1}{4}$-inch drill is adequate for this purpose. Alternatively short strips of brass or stainless steel may be bent to a suitable U-shape and screwed to the gunwale strips. If you use the latter method smooth the edges of the metal strips before fixing or your painter may become frayed just when it is most needed!

Glasspaper the outside of the canoe and varnish it with

Plate 9 (*opposite*) Foredeck fixed.

36

Figure 10 Seat/
floorboard/
footrest unit.

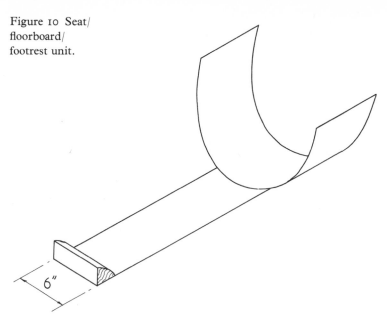

6"

two or three coats; rubbing down between coats with 'wet
or dry' paper used wet. This is a special type of abrasive
paper which is particularly good for smoothing varnish or
paintwork. To use it wet, dip the paper into water and rub
it on a piece of soap. When the surface clogs it can be washed
clean. Leave the hull to dry after using the wet paper and
before applying the next coat of varnish.

While the varnish is drying you can make up your seat/
floorboard/footrest unit which should be made to fit you.
Do not fix the footrest yet for you will want to obtain the
most comfortable position when you are sitting in your
canoe. For a start you will find the curved plywood seat plus
a piece of foam rubber (securely glued on) quite adequate,
but for long trips you may decide to buy or make a moulded
glass-fibre seat which can be screwed to your floorboard. The
sides of the curved plywood seat should fit closely against
your hips to prevent you slipping sideways if you lean the
canoe. If the seat is too wide for you fix spacing pieces at the
sides where the seat touches the coaming supports. Varnish
the seat unit and your canoe is completed.

The unit can be screwed to the keelson and coaming

supports or fastened by means of turn-buttons – this is the better arrangement as it makes cleaning the interior easier. Position the unit so that the bows of the canoe are just slightly higher than the stern when you are sitting in it.

Materials list for the canoe

Hull and deck	Two sheets 3-mm marine plywood 8 feet × 4 feet
Gunwale strips	Two pieces 15 feet × $\frac{7}{8}$ inches × $\frac{5}{8}$ inches spruce or similar
Keelson	One piece 8 feet × 3 inches × $\frac{1}{2}$ inch spruce or similar
Coaming supports	Two pieces 2 feet 9 inches × $\frac{7}{8}$ inches × $\frac{5}{8}$ inches spruce or similar
Keel strip	One piece 9 feet × $\frac{3}{4}$ inches half round moulding
Frames and blocks	One piece 2 feet × 1 foot × $\frac{1}{2}$ inch (12 mm) marine plywood

One pack of waterproof resin glue such as Cascamite One-Shot or Aerolite 306.

Two gross $\frac{5}{8}$ inch × 16 S.W.G. Gripfast boat nails for keelson and deck.

Four ounces $\frac{3}{4}$-inch brass panel pins (or $\frac{5}{8}$-inch serrated shoe brads) for hull to gunwale strips, coaming *etc.*

One fibre-glass kit consisting of 1-inch wide tape, resin, catalyst and hardener.

A number of $2\frac{1}{2}$-inch lengths of 18 S.W.G. copper wire which may be cut from appropriate electrical wire or bought ready cut from a canoe kit supplier.

One quart of marine grade varnish – the minimum quantity you will need.

Except for the keelson the timber sizes are overlength to allow for fitting. The seat and floorboard are made from hull and deck offcuts.

Tools list

Soft pencil.
2-foot rule or steel tape measure.

Marking gauge – can be home-made as described.
Tenon or fine-toothed panel saw.
Coping saw.
Smoothing or 'Surform' plane.
Spokeshave.
Hand drill.
$\frac{1}{4}$-inch twist drill.
Hammer.
Screwdriver.
Pincers and pliers.
Two sash cramps or Spanish windlass.
Two 6-inch G-cramps.
Varnish brush.
Resin brush.

3   Some accessories to make

Regardless of the type of canoeing you intend to enjoy, a paddle suited to the task is essential. The paddle is a personal piece of equipment which should suit both you and your canoe. The overall length is dependent upon the beam of your canoe and your own height – a very beamy canoe will obviously require a longer paddle then a narrow racing canoe. Similarly if you are short you may find a long paddle somewhat unwieldy to handle. The factors involving size of paddler and canoe have been considered far more recently by canoe manufacturers, some of whom are now producing short, narrow craft especially for the young paddler. Despite all these points you will probably find a paddle of about seven feet overall length perfectly satisfactory for use with the canoe described in Chapter Two.

Another important consideration is the weight of the paddle. This depends upon the type of wood used and for a spruce and plywood one a weight of about two pounds is usual. The question of weight will impress its importance on you during a tour when you may be holding the paddle for several hours each day. Construction of a simple touring paddle is not difficult and, if you have already built your *DK 12* canoe, quite inexpensive since you will be able to use the offcuts of plywood from the deck for the blades.

For the shaft you will need a piece of straight grained spruce, 7 feet long by $1\frac{1}{4}$-inches square. Before you mark out the shaft for planing it will be necessary to decide on how you want the blades set. Canoeists have the blades of their paddles set at right angles so the blade which is travelling forward through the air is 'feathered' to reduce wind resistance. Some paddlers control the feather with the left hand, some with the right. To determine which control suits you try making paddling motions with your future paddle shaft – or even a broomstick! Left-hand control, which is normal for most right-handed canoeists, means that the left hand does the turning of the shaft to produce the feather while the right hand allows the shaft to twist. If left-hand control seems natural to you the blade on the right will be in the paddling position when the blade on the left has its face downwards. Right-hand control merely involves having the left-hand blade facing upwards in the same situation.

Making the paddle is straightforward – begin by shaping the shaft. Mark the length of the blades on the two sides where they will be fixed. Leaving these two sections flat start by planing off the edges and continue until the shaft is round. Do not plane the sides of the sections where the blades will be. Mark the centre between the end of the shaft and the line defining the inner end of the blades. At this centre mark down the sides $\frac{3}{8}$ inch. This point defines the curvature of the blade and the curve can now be drawn as shown on figure 11. Remove the waste with a spokeshave; round the ends of the shaft a little and thin down the part which will be supporting the blades as shown.

Figure 11 Paddle shaft showing end shape.

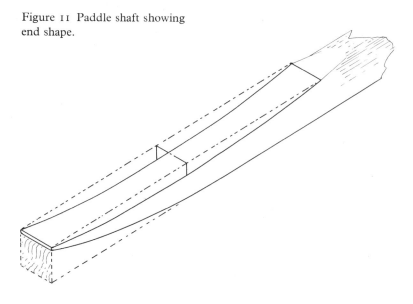

The shaft is now ready to receive the blades which are marked out on the plywood from the details given on figure 12. Cut out the blades using a coping or fret saw, smooth the edges with a spokeshave and they are ready to fix. Glue and pin them into place.

When the blades are fixed and the glue set the whole paddle can be glasspapered and varnished. Before varnishing you may like to strengthen the blades by glass-taping across the ends. This adds little to the weight and does help prevent the blades splitting. You may also like to paint your blades a distinctive colour to aid identification or perhaps in your canoe club colours.

Although you now have your canoe and paddle there are a few more items of equipment which you will need before venturing on to the local river or canal. Two of these can be made at home and will be decribed first; the others must be bought and will be dealt with in the next chapter.

The most essential of the two items you can make is the spray cover; this might be described as a mini-skirt elastic fastened around your waist at the top and around the cockpit coaming at the bottom. Its purpose is to keep water out of the canoe be it rain, spray or even waves. It follows

44

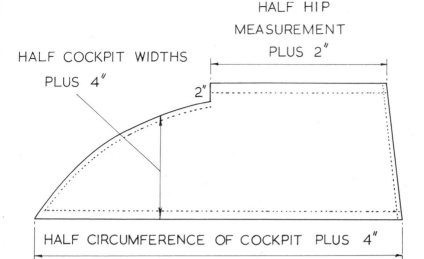

HALF HIP MEASUREMENT PLUS 2"

HALF COCKPIT WIDTHS PLUS 4"

2"

HALF CIRCUMFERENCE OF COCKPIT PLUS 4"

Figure 13 Approximate shape of one side of the spray cover.

that it must be a good fit both on you and the canoe if it is to do its job satisfactorily. The method I describe for making a spray cover does not pretend to be original but it is one I have used and found reasonably easy. I have not given actual dimensions on the drawing for, inevitably, your cockpit will not be quite the same shape as mine. Indeed you may not want it the same shape, but if you follow the instructions you will finish with an adequate spray cover.

Basically the spray cover is going to consist of two pieces of waterproof material sewn together. The only difficulty is in determining the shape of the two pieces which will be identical but left- and right-handed. The way to overcome this is to first make one side using a piece of cheap material or even paper if you are careful with it. This material must be as long as half the perimeter of the cockpit plus an allowance for a seam at each end and a little spare which will be taken up by the elastic, say a total allowance of 4 inches. The width of the material must be half the width of the cockpit taken over the coaming plus allowances as shown on figure 13.

Figure 12 (*opposite*) Paddle blade.

Plate 11 Folded trolley.

Having determined the shape of one side cut out two such sides from your waterproof material, making sure you have one left- and one right-hand side. Sew the two pieces together at the back seam then hem the top and bottom for the elastic and finally sew the front seam starting and finishing inside the hem, i.e. do not oversew the hem. Thread your elastic through and the cover is complete. The threading may prove difficult with some kinds of waterproof material and you will probably find it best to first thread a piece of thin cord and use this to pull through the elastic. As a safeguard knot a loop at the end of the elastic in the bottom hem so that in the unlikely event of the cover jamming on the canoe you will be able to pull it off with the loop.

The second item which you can make is by no means essential but is a useful accessory if you live within walking

46

Plate 12 Trolley in use.

distance of canoeing water or if you do a tour where there are portages of more than a few yards. It is the folding trolley. These may be bought from canoe suppliers, but they are also simple and inexpensive to make.

The drawing, figure 14, is really self-explanatory but I will describe briefly the construction procedure. Make up the two wheel arms first; cut one end of each at an angle of 45 degrees and glue on the axle blocks. Leave the arms over-length at this stage. When the glue is set bore the holes for the axle bolts which must be a tight fit. The blocks may then be shaped as shown. Make up the centre beam and bore the holes in the positions shown. Use a piece of scrap wood as a spacer when boring these and ensure that they are at right angles to the beam. If they are not it may be necessary to enlarge them a little with a file to prevent the wheel arm

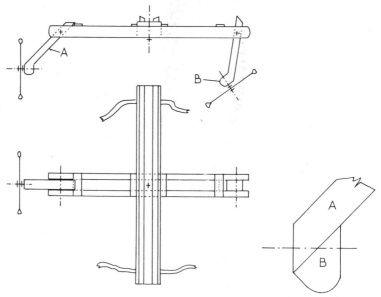

Figure 14 Folding trolley.

fouling when it is folded. Bore the second hole in each wheel arm $6\frac{1}{2}$ inches from the axle bolt hole. Bolt the arms into the centre beam and fit the axle bolts.

Place the frame on the bench and splay the arms until the axle bolts are $\frac{1}{4}$ inch lower at their outer ends. Put the stops in place against the arms and mark their positions. Unbolt the frame and pin and glue the stops in place.

Make the keel support and the two shaped pieces to suit the canoe. Bore holes in the centre of the support and the centre block and bolt them together. Pin and glue the locating pieces into place each side of the keel support. Cut the wheel arms to length and angled as shown for neatness.

Glasspaper all marks off and give the trolley two coats of marine quality varnish. Finally fix the two holding straps with a piece of thin plywood under the screws to prevent them pulling through, and your trolley is ready for the first portage!

48

Materials list for trolley

Centre beam block	One piece $3 \times 1\frac{3}{8} \times 1\frac{3}{8}$ inches
Centre beam	Two pieces $24 \times 1\frac{3}{8} \times \frac{7}{8}$ inches
Stops	Two pieces $3\frac{1}{4} \times 1\frac{3}{8} \times \frac{1}{4}$ inches
Locating pieces	Two pieces $3\frac{1}{4} \times \frac{7}{8} \times \frac{1}{4}$ inches
Keel support	One piece $24 \times 3 \times \frac{1}{2}$ inches
Shaped pieces	Two pieces $24 \times \frac{5}{8} \times \frac{5}{8}$ inches
Wheel arms	Two pieces $9 \times 1\frac{3}{8} \times \frac{7}{8}$ inches
Axle blocks	Two pieces $2 \times 1\frac{3}{8} \times \frac{7}{8}$ inches

Two brass bolts for the axles with four nuts, length and diameter to suit the wheels.

Two $\frac{1}{4}$-inch diameter 4-inch brass bolts with four nuts.

One $\frac{1}{4}$-inch diameter $2\frac{1}{2}$-inch brass bolt with one wing nut.

Five $\frac{1}{4}$-inch inside diameter brass washers.

Two straps to suit the canoe.

Two wheels of between 6 and 8-inch diameter.

Waterproof glue and brass pins.

4   More essentials

The remaining three items of equipment you will need are some form of buoyancy for your canoe, a life-jacket for yourself and one or two painters for the canoe. Buoyancy for the canoe is absolutely essential for although a wooden canoe will float it will be very difficult to handle if it becomes full of water and recovery is hampered. A canoe made from glass-reinforced plastics will not float when full of water and in this case buoyancy is even more important.

The simplest type of buoyancy is cheapest and perhaps best; it is simply an inflated bag pushed firmly into each end of the canoe and preferably fixed there. A useful type of bag, if you can get it, is the one in which bulk vinegar is sold. These bags are protected by a thick cardboard box for their normal use but removed from this they make ideal buoyancy bags. They have a plastic tap which facilitates inflation and is air-tight. A similar bag can also be bought if a free supply cannot be found!

Rather more expensive are specially shaped bags which fit neatly into the ends of the canoe and have a long tube for ease of inflation. All inflated forms of buoyancy have the disadvantage that they are liable to leak, possibly without you knowing until it is too late. It is also almost impossible to make a satisfactory repair to a plastic bag.

More permanent buoyancy can be obtained by glueing into the canoe blocks of expanded polystyrene or by mixing together the two ingredients of polyurethane foam and allowing it to form in the ends of the canoe. This latter method has its dangers for the foaming could be so great that it forces the deck off!

Lastly it is possible to build air-tight compartments into the ends of the canoe but this is usually more difficult than it sounds; very often the compartment will leak which means that eventually water gets in and the unventilated space will offer ideal conditions for rot to begin. I am in favour of air bags – have what you like but do have some form of buoyancy in your canoe.

You will also need personal buoyancy if you are going to venture onto anything other than a shallow stream in summer. A life-jacket is an immense help in the event of an accidental capsize for it enables you to collect your thoughts, the paddle and the canoe without having to worry about supporting yourself. It is especially important to wear a life-jacket if the water is cold, or you are tired, on your own or on the sea. The photographs in this book show a canoeist wearing a type of life-jacket which is approved by the British Canoe Union. It has two types of buoyancy, blocks of foam for normal use providing over 20 lbs of buoyancy plus inflation to provide full life-jacket buoyancy of over 40 lbs. A life-jacket of this type will keep your face above water even if you become unconscious – and this can happen surprisingly quickly in cold water.

The final item for the canoe is the painter – or better still – two painters, one for each end. The painter is a piece of strong line – $\frac{1}{2}$-inch circumference nylon or terylene is fine – securely fastened to the end of the canoe. I am in favour of knotting them using a bowline, they are then easily removed for other purposes if required. Each painter should be about the length of the canoe and when not in use should be tied to each other to form a life-line on both sides of the canoe.

The painter has many uses the most obvious of which is to moor the canoe. It is also used for lining down shallow rapids (or rough ones); this is rather like taking the dog for a walk. It may sometimes be necessary to utilise it as a means of lifting the canoe out of the water, e.g. up a high bank. It may even double as a clothes line but an old clothes line cannot double as a painter!

Now we are ready at last to start our canoeing. You should be wearing shorts, as anything else will get wet and drip round your legs; old plimsoles or sandals to protect your feet from

the inevitable broken bottles and rubbish which finds its way into our rivers; a shirt or sweater and if it is cold or wet an anorak. The anorak should be a proper waterproof one, not the 'showerproof' variety which will leak after a very short time. The waterproof one will make you damp from perspiration but this is better than being both wet and cold from rain or spray.

Rubber boots of any design are deadly in a canoe – they are liable to trap your feet in the canoe or, if they allow you out, they will promptly pull you beneath the water. Basketball boots on the other hand are useful in very rocky conditions as they offer protection to your ankles. It goes without saying, I hope, that you must be prepared for any of this clothing to get wet!

Canoeing is very much an individual sport and I am going to assume that you will be using a single-seat canoe at this stage. Certainly it is easier to learn in a single where you have only yourself to bother about. Most of the strokes I shall describe can be performed in a double and some of the pros and cons of doubles will be considered later.

Let us assume you have arrived at your local river with your canoe and it is lying on the bank gleaming in the warm sunshine. Look at the bank of the river and find a place where it is firm and about one foot above the water level. You will need at least six inches of water to float the canoe and check too there are no snags or rubbish to cause damage.

Pick up your canoe by taking hold of the coaming at the point of balance, roughly in the middle. Place the canoe on the bank parallel to the river with the bow facing upstream. Have the paddle on the bank within reach but not where you will tread on it. To launch the canoe pick it up by the coaming – hold the bow painter in one hand – and put the canoe into the water. If the launching space is restricted by trees or bushes launch the canoe stern first. To do this put the canoe down on the bank with the stern out over the water, lift the bows until the stern is in the water and the whole canoe is off the bank. Then with the bow painter

Plate 13 (*opposite*) Hilary and her canoe.

firmly held, push the canoe into the river and allow the current to carry the stern downstream, as the canoe comes parallel to the bank lower the bows into the water.

Always start and finish facing upstream as the canoe is easier to control in this position. To remove the canoe from the water use either launching method in reverse, the second method being the easier.

Getting into the canoe from the low bank requires care if you are to stay in. Place your paddle across the front of the cockpit with the outer blade flat over the water. Hold the paddle onto the coaming with your left hand (assuming the canoe is on your left), put your left foot into the centre of the canoe but keep your weight on your right foot and right hand which will be placed firmly on the bank. Transfer your weight to the canoe placing your right foot in front of your left on the centre line of the canoe and at the same time sit down. Your right hand will still be holding you to the bank. The essential point to grasp is that of getting down onto the seat as soon as your weight is in the canoe. If the canoe does tip outwards the flat of the paddle hitting the water will slow the movement sufficiently for you to sit down and recover your balance. To get out of the canoe reverse this procedure.

If there is no suitable bank you may have to get into the canoe from shallow water. In this case the procedure is similar, but both hands hold the coaming; you sit down before your second foot is in the canoe, and bring your second foot into the cockpit after you are seated. Shake the the water from your feet before putting them in the cockpit. When getting out into shallow water make sure it *is* shallow. Many streams have very uneven bottoms and you may feel your canoe scraping over stones but by the time you have a foot over the side the depth has increased to three feet! I mention this because although it is possible to get out into deep water there is usually no need to and doing so unintentionally can be dampening – I write from experience gained on a well-known mill stream near the Thames.

Plate 14 (*opposite above*) Sideways launch.
Plate 15 (*opposite*) Stern launch.

It is possible to paddle with both legs over the sides of the cockpit and if you are canoeing a small stream with many shallows this does enable you to get your weight out of the canoe quickly – but do keep hold of the stern painter or you may wave goodbye to your canoe as it slides away between your legs.

Do not be worried if the canoe feels positively unsafe even when you are sitting down. This is a normal first reaction and you will rapidly gain confidence. If you are tempted to make or buy a very tubby canoe with the idea that it will be safer you will almost certainly find it too 'stodgy' once you have gained a little experience. Canoeing has something in common with horse riding in that you and the canoe must – like horse and rider – work together; this is only possible if you fit firmly into a seat which in turn is fixed to the canoe. Your feet should rest against a footrest otherwise your legs will not be helping the forward progress of the canoe. Knees

Plate 16 Getting in from a low bank.

can either rest against the inside of the coaming or be pressed up just under the coaming. The position you adopt rather depends upon your shape but in any case you may find it worthwhile to glue pieces of foam rubber to the coaming where you touch it. For some strokes it is necessary to fit bars or shaped brackets under which you can brace your thighs. Fittings such as these are essential for Eskimo rolling or you would simply fall out of the cockpit.

It is just possible that you may have already capsized but if you have not this will be a good place to explain what to do in such an event. The first point to remember is that capsizing in itself is not a catastrophe. Recovery of the canoe is greatly simplified if it is left inverted after the capsize; if you attempt to right the canoe in deep water it will probably fill up and become very difficult to handle.

Let us assume you have capsized completely and have just surfaced on the far side of your canoe. The canoe will be

Plate 17 Getting in from shallow water.

Plate 18 Emptying the canoe.

floating quite happily in its inverted position and will support you too if required to do so; leave the canoe inverted.

If you have lost hold of your paddle recover it before it floats out of reach and swim with the canoe to the nearest bank. Swimming with a canoe is not the easiest of tasks so take the shortest route to the bank; do not worry about being swept downstream unless you know of some danger such as a weir. In this case get to the bank fast even if it means abandoning the canoe. It is sometimes easier to swim to the bank with the end of the painter and pull the canoe to you when in shallow water. Should the bank be unsuitable for landing allow yourself to drift with the canoe until a suitable place presents itself. In a rapid river drift feet first holding on to the upstream end of the canoe – your feet will then hit any rocks before your head!

The ideal bank is gently sloping with a shelving bottom of sand. Land and put your paddle out of harm's way and with

58

one end of the canoe in the shallow water near the bank gently raise and twist the other end; this will break the air-lock which exists inside the canoe and allow some of the water to run out. When no more water runs out turn the canoe over. Now push the end of the canoe down so the remaining water runs into the end nearest you and with a single movement lift the end and turn the canoe over. Any water still in the canoe after this can be sponged out.

It is possible to carry out this emptying procedure in deeper water but it is then slightly more difficult. If you have a companion, as you should of course, he or she can take the place of the river and you simply raise and lower the ends until all the water is out. What you must avoid at all costs is trying to lift the canoe, or one end of it, when it has a lot of water inside. It you are able to lift it you will either break its back or the water will rip off the deck in making its escape.

If you are worried about getting stuck in the cockpit try capsizing deliberately when you have some assistance to hand. This is a good confidence builder and is part of the BCU Proficiency Test which is a useful pointer to your personal ability in a canoe.

5   On the water

Now you can sit in your canoe quite confidently you can begin paddling. Once you have mastered the principle of feathering the double-bladed paddle its use for forward and backward paddling is very simple.

Push away from the bank – use your hand not the paddle – and begin paddling. Hold the paddle shaft with your hands a little further apart than the width of your shoulders; most beginners have a tendency to grip the shaft too tightly with their hands too close together. A fairly relaxed grip is all that is necessary.

Reach forward with your right hand and twist your right shoulder a little forward too. Put the right blade in the water without splashing, as near the canoe as possible and pull it back through the water pushing forward at the same time with your left hand. Your left foot should also be pushing against the footrest. When the right blade is just past your body take it from the water and twist the left blade into position for its stroke. As you pull with your left hand your right foot presses against the footrest. Paddle gently at this stage, sit up and relax. Do not try to go fast but avoid looking at the paddle blades, rocking the canoe or moving your body unnecessarily.

Paddling backwards is exactly the reverse of forward paddling. The blade is put into the water by your hip and pushed forward. Use the *back* of the blade, i.e. have them facing the same way as for forward paddling. This is to enable you to change from one to the other with least effort. Use back paddling as a brake.

To turn, as for a bend in a river, either pull harder on one side which will have the effect of turning the front of the canoe away from that side, or paddle on one side only for a

Plate 19 (*opposite*) Forward paddling.

Plate 20 (*opposite*) Backward paddling.

Plate 21 A sweep stroke.

few strokes. In this latter case keep to your normal paddling rhythm but let the blade on the inside of the bend skim the surface of the water. These methods are suitable for gentle bends or turns but if you have to turn in the width of a narrow river other methods must be used.

One way is to combine forward and back paddling on opposite sides of the canoe. For a right turn pull the left blade back through the water and instead of letting the right blade dip into the water for its stroke bring it back and push it forward through the water. This is repeated until the desired turn is completed.

A slightly more advanced method is to use a *sweep* stroke. Instead of putting the blades into the water near the canoe and pulling straight back the blade is pulled through the water so as to describe an arc from the front of the canoe to the back with your shoulder at the centre. The blade is put into the water facing away from the canoe and is gradually twisted through 180 degrees until it is facing the canoe at the

62

Plate 22 A low telemark turn.

end of the stroke. This may also be done in combination,
forward one side, backwards on the other.

The last type of turn is the *telemark turn* which takes its
name from a skiing turn. To perform a telemark it is
necessary to be moving forward at a reasonable speed; put
one blade on the water behind your body position, back
down, with its leading edge angled slightly upwards. Lean on
this blade and sweep it forward on top of the water. With
practice you will be able to make very fast turns using this
stroke. It is the initial leaning on the paddle blade which
provides most of the turning effect; the forward movement
is the recovery action necessary to prevent a capsize.

Mention of a capsize leads us to another pair of strokes
which can prevent an impending ducking. The first of these
is *support sculling* which involves moving the blade rapidly
back and forth on top of the water always with its leading
edge raised, i.e. the back edge becomes the leading edge when
the blade changes direction. This stroke will provide

63

sufficient support for you to be able to get your shoulder wet on the side you are performing the stroke. Keep the paddle low while doing this stroke and twist the shaft with the hand nearest to the water. Sculling is a particularly good confidence builder.

A more dynamic stroke is the *slap support*, a most useful stroke for rapid recovery of balance. To practise the slap support lean the canoe until you feel you are going to capsize and slap the flat of the paddle blade down on the water in line with your body and as far out as you can comfortably reach. As the blade hits the water you will be able to push yourself up against the resistance of the water under the blade. It is essential to do this stroke very whole-heartedly – a timid attempt will result in failure and a ducking.

Lastly there are two similar strokes which we can utilise for moving the canoe sideways – a requirement more often needed than you may think! The *draw stroke* is like the slap support in that it must be done firmly without dithering. It

Plate 23 Sculling for support.

provides the quickest method of moving the canoe bodily sideways – useful if you round a corner on a fast stream to find most of the river blocked by a fallen tree. To perform the draw stroke reach out to one side with the blade which is going into the water parallel to the canoe. Keep the paddle as near vertical as you can, which means having the upper arm extended; lean the canoe, put the blade in the water and pull it towards you very rapidly. Withdraw the blade by slicing it out toward the bow or stern before it gets under the hull of the canoe. Once the paddle is under the canoe it is very easy to pull yourself over. Practise so this does not happen.

The same stroke may be modified slightly to move the canoe at an angle by simply making the stroke nearer the bow or stern according to the way you wish to go.

The other method of moving sideways is by *sculling*. Again it is necessary to hold the paddle vertical but this time the blade is moved back and forth in the water using the

Plate 24 Slap support.

Plate 25 Draw stroke.

Plate 26 Sculling draw.

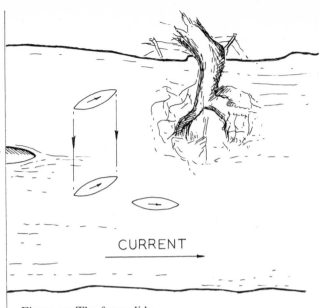

CURRENT

Figure 15 The ferry glide.

lower hand to twist the blade so that the leading edge is always angled away from the canoe. This is a useful stroke when in a confined space, e.g. a slalom gate.

For all the strokes your hands retain their normal grip and position on the paddle shaft; it is then possible to combine a number of different strokes to suit any situation as it occurs. Do practise them all on *both* sides of the canoe.

The last item in this collection of strokes is not really a stroke but a technique known as the *ferry glide*. This is a method of moving sideways while retaining full control over the forward or backward movement of the canoe. Its main use is to give you time to take a look at ('survey') an obstacle such as a bridge with fallen masonry blocking its arches. It works best on rivers flowing at a reasonable rate, over three knots say, because it is the force of the current which moves the canoe sideways. If you are paddling downstream and arrive at an obstacle without an obvious solution angle your canoe slightly *against* the direction in which you wish to go and back paddle just hard enough to hold the canoe stationary relative to the bank. The current will then move you sideways in the direction the stern of the canoe is pointing.

68

If you want to move to the left bank the front of the canoe must be angled towards the right bank. To move back in the opposite direction change the angle of the canoe. If you are travelling upstream, angle in the opposite direction, i.e. the canoe will move in the direction toward which the bow is angled. The faster the water if flowing the smaller the angle required. You must of course decide before any hazard is reached whether or not you are going to be able to hold the canoe against the current – if not get to the bank in good time and survey from the land. If you have any doubts about your ability to cope with the difficulty avoid it by taking your canoe out and portaging round.

6 Pottering in your canoe

If you begin your canoeing alone instead of joining a club you may at first find yourself limited to day trips on a local river. Depending on its size you will almost certainly meet other users and it is with the idea of making waterways congenial places for all those who use them that the Central Council of Physical Recreation has drawn up a Water Sports Code. The Code offers recommendations for all users of inland waterways to minimise interference of one sport by the participants of another.

The main snag so far as canoeing is concerned is the fact that most English and Welsh rivers are private. The owner of the banks of a river also owns the rights to that part of the river flowing past his land. The rights may of course be disposed of to fishing clubs or other groups. For this reason a number of the better known fishing rivers are closed to canoeists except by arrangement with the BCU who may be able to obtain permission for the river to be canoed during the close fishing season. For fly fishing this is between October and the end of February, and for coarse fishing, March to mid-June.

Fortunately this is not the full story or canoeing might well have ceased as an outdoor sport long ago. You are legally allowed a right of passage on the tidal parts of rivers and on those rivers where there is a statutory right to navigate. These include the Severn, Wye, Trent, Great Ouse and Thames but not necessarily the whole river in each case.

Other rivers such as the Lea and Stort may be useable because they have been made into navigations and their flow is controlled by weirs.

An important point to note is that the right, where it exists, is to 'navigate'; this does not mean that you are automatically allowed to land or moor to the banks. On the rivers mentioned this does not present undue difficulties except for parts of the Wye and upper Severn. Here again the BCU will be able to help you and further details are given in the last chapter.

The Thames is an expensive river on which to canoe for it is necessary to buy an annual licence costing £1 and you will also have to pay to go 'through, by or over' each lock. There are a few exceptions to the licence payment for racing and members of some groups and clubs. Parts of the Thames, especially above Oxford, are very pleasant but it is mostly a rather busy river much populated by small motor boats. If you want to 'do' the Thames there is a strip map available which also gives details of the several small streams which join loops of the main river. Most of these are good fun and well worth taking in place of the main stream.

I am not going to give a list of canoeable rivers; others have already done this most efficiently and another list would be out of place in a book such as this.

For messing about in boats there is perhaps no better way than pottering in a canoe along some backwater, deserted but for the dart of colour that is the kingfisher and an occasional cow, knee deep in water and mud. These small streams, delightful as they are, often have hidden dangers for the canoeist – not the cow, a ferry glide will take care of her. It is the debris of civilisation which may cause trouble. I have found an old bed frame dumped in a stream which was apparently miles from anywhere; it is objects of this kind which can, without the warning of a rapid or weir, puncture your canoe or give you a ducking. I have already mentioned the broken glass and similar small rubbish which can be so dangerous in shallow waters where you may have to do some walking. Unfortunately it is very necessary to be aware of these things and to take precautions where they are likely to be present.

Another of the gentle aspects of canoeing is that of canal touring. Many of our canals are in remote parts of the country where you can go all day without seeing another human being. Canals are of course man-made and have no current except that which may be induced when a lock is filled at the lower end of a section (or 'pound'). The water in them is supplied by feeder streams and the locks are the means of raising the canal over hills in its path. In some places aqueducts carry the canal across the valley between the hills! Since there is no current it is not necessary to have a weir to control the flow.

On the canals and some rivers (such as parts of the Great Ouse) you will have to work the locks yourself. You will need a suitable lock key – not really a key but a large winch handle used for opening the sluices in the lock gates. The key may be bought or perhaps hired for the duration of the tour; every year many disappear forever into the mud at the bottom of some lock so make sure yours is either safe on the bank or in the canoe when it is not being used. I can also remember very vividly the occasion when I had a two mile walk back to the last lock for the key I had forgotten; be warned!

Use of the lock is simple; they usually consist of two pairs of gates which come together to form a V pointing upstream or to the highest level so the water pressure keeps them closed. Some types of lock have one pair of gates, usually the downstream pair, replaced by an iron gate which is moved vertically to allow the craft to pass.

If you are travelling from the lower to the higher level and the lock is full, moor your canoe clear of the gates to avoid damage when the water in the lock is released. Close the gates at the upper end and check that the sluices or 'slackers' are closed; these may be in the gates or in the sides of the lock itself. This seals off the lock from the upper level. Open the lower sluices to empty the lock to the level of the lower section. It is only necessary to open one sluice or in the case of the vertical iron gate, to open it about six inches until the levels coincide. When the levels are the same, you can open the gates by leaning on the beam extending over the bank from the top of the gate. Paddle into the lock or, if you are alone, pull your canoe in and secure it back and front to the chains or bollards on the lock wall. The quick release version of the sheet bend is a useful knot here.

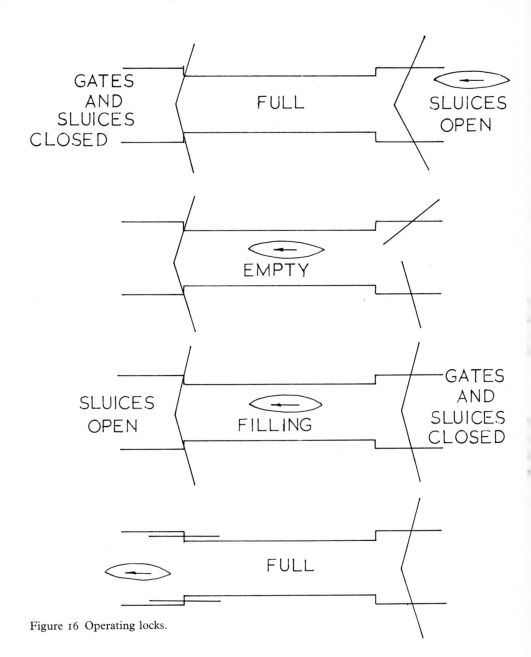

Figure 16 Operating locks.

Close the lower gates and sluices and open the upper sluices. As the water level rises control your canoe by manipulating the painters. Again it is sufficient usually to open only one sluice and even that rather gradually for considerable turbulence can be caused; as the lock fills this will lessen and the sluice may be opened further to speed the process. When the lock is full the upper gates can be opened and your canoe pulled out. Close all sluices before you leave unless other instructions are given on the lock.

At first sight the lock may appear a frightening place but if normal commonsense prevails there is no danger to the canoeist. If there are a lot of enthusiatic helpers ready to close or open gates make sure your canoe does not get caught between them – it would be crushed like an eggshell. Once in the lock avoid the ends for there are sometimes ledges which are apparent only when the lock is empty and to get partially caught on one of these could mean a wetting. Should this happen either wait until the lock is full or if, as is more likely, it is emptying until the lower gates are open and get out onto the lock wall or a convenient bank. Hold onto your canoe and if possible something on the lock wall while you are waiting. There are often chains hanging in vertical grooves in the lock wall. Another reason for staying in the middle of the lock is the fountain of water which may come through a gap between the upper gates. In an ill-kept lock this can be quite a considerable jet of water. Lastly avoid going into a lock with larger craft, as you stand far too much chance of being crushed.

Locks on rivers are usually situated somewhere near a weir which will incorporate a method of controlling the flow of water. The weir is simply a wall which retains a certain head of water, when the water rises above this level it flows over the weir. Normally arranged as part of the weir or next to it are sluice gates which can be opened or closed to control the flow of water into the lower level. Control is particularly necessary in times of flood or drought.

The danger from weirs is small if the canoeist takes normal care. There is no danger of being swept over – you will see or hear the weir in ample time to take avoiding action. Some weirs are shootable but there is more to this than merely pointing the canoe in the right direction and they are best left alone at this stage.

Preparations for a day trip should be as careful and complete as those for a three week tour. A change of clothing including something warm like a sweater are essential for yourself and a suitable repair kit for the canoe; further details on repair kits are given later. The two painters should be checked; a spare line about twice as long as the canoe will also be found useful at times and should be carried in an accessible place but not where it can become coiled around your legs in the event of a capsize. You will of course have buoyancy at each end and preferably a spray cover although this is not essential on most lowland rivers or canals.

Items such as the clothing and perhaps the repair kit must be packed in waterproof bags. For day trips the stronger type of plastic bag is suitable but for camping tours a tougher bag is needed and these may be bought or made from the same material as the spray cover. Seams can be taped or a lighter plastic bag used inside to ensure complete protection. Now you are ready to venture out on your local water I emphasise my earlier advice: join a club.

7   Canoe touring and camping

Canoes have always been used for travelling and provide an ideal method of seeing the countryside in a new light. As most rivers go into remote country for at least part of their length it is usually necessary to camp when canoe touring. Normally you will carry all your equipment in the canoe, not something to create a problem in these days of sophisticated lightweight camping equipment. It is possible to canoe from a standing camp and arrange for a non-canoeing member of the group to transport the canoeing party back to the camp at the end of the day. This system will be discussed in more detail when I deal with group canoeing.

The first requirement of a canoe tour is the canoeing water and the easiest way to determine this is to consult a waterways guide such as that published by the BCU or the one written by Percy Blandford (see Chapter 12). The guide will give river gradings so you will be able to choose one suited to your experience. If possible try to visit the river before the tour to check on the starting point – if you have had a long journey you may wish to camp for the first night before getting under way; is there a suitable site nearby? Similarly it is worth checking the place where you are going to finish the tour. It is usually difficult to arrange camp sites along a route – you will be forever concerned about making up time to arrive at the next site and so on, this is no way to enjoy a canoe cruise the whole essence of which is its carefree nature. If you know, or have been told, that sites are difficult to find along some stretch of river by all means try to find suitable ones before you arrive. In this case allow plenty of time and treat the arrival day at the arranged site as a rest day or perhaps for shopping or sightseeing.

Transport to the start is best by car and roof rack for the

individual or pair of canoeists. The car can be left at the start and the driver returns by bus or train on the last day to collect it. Failing a car of your own you will have to persuade your father or a friend to transport you and your canoe – you may have to provide the roof rack of course!

As your camping will be incidental to the canoeing you will need only the bare essentials for producing adequate food and shelter. It is possible to camp without a tent and this can be good fun but do not be tempted to try it for your first cruise. After a day of paddling in the rain you will be only too pleased to have a simple lightweight tent in which you can keep warm and dry.

The tent then is the first priority and as it is to be used mainly for overnight shelter it can be both simple and small. Simplicity here refers to the ease of erecting the tent, it may be quite a complicated looking thing if it is a modern one pole type but these are very easy to erect even if you are tired and wet. Of course the tent does not have to be of this type; the small ridge tent is perfectly adequate if it is made from tent cloth and waterproofed. Tent cloth should be finely woven stuff and the proofing is of the kind which leaves the cloth looking much the same but probably coloured. Avoid tents which have any form of wax proofing, this soon wears out and is then useless. If you can afford only a white, unproofed tent it is easy to apply your own proofing which is obtainable in the form of a liquid which can be brushed on or if the tent is sufficiently small it can be dipped in a bucket.

A groundsheet which fits the floor space of the tent is essential. This sheet must be completely waterproof and the best sort are made of material impregnated with plastics. There are arguments for and against having the groundsheet sewn into the tent. Personally I feel this is unnecessary and you are likely to get mud onto the tent from the groundsheet. However, against this is a more draughtproof and insect proof tent – you can make your own choice. A cheap tent can easily have its groundsheet sewn in if you feel it is worthwhile.

Now as your tent is likely to be small and with only

Plate 27 The 'Good Companions Minor' single pole tent.

sitting headroom you are almost bound to touch the sides when moving inside it. If you do this during rain the tent will leak where it has been touched; it is also likely to let in a fine spray during heavy rain – this will happen with the best quality lightweight tent and is normal. Both these wet weather snags can be eliminated by means of a flysheet. In effect the flysheet is a second tent which fits over the tent proper with an airspace between them. The flysheet normally has no doors but often has a short extension which provides a porch to keep rain off the doors of the tent. A simple ridge tent flysheet can be made from two lengths of unbleached cotton sheeting which can be proofed after making up. The main job of the flysheet is to break the fall of the rain drops before they hit the tent; if it comes close to the ground and has a porch so much the better for it can then be used for storing those items which cannot be harmed by damp.

Tent poles and pegs are made from a variety of materials but generally speaking the canoeist wants the lightest; for a single pole tent aluminium alloy is the best but for the small ridge tent, perhaps 3 feet 6 inches high, the wooden poles which are usually supplied are quite satisfactory. Pegs should be of the skewer type either steel or alloy, the weight difference is little but the alloy type will not rust.

The next essential is a sleeping bag; it is possible to make do with blankets but for comfort buy the best sleeping bag you can afford. Synthetic bags filled with terylene or similar materials are available but these are bulky compared with a down-filled bag and for the present at least the down-filled bag is the best bet for the canoeist. Do try to afford the best quality for with care the bag will last a long time and the best quality down makes a far warmer bag than the cheapest. Use a cotton lining in the sleeping bag; this is well worth the little extra weight for the protection it gives the bag and for hygiene.

What you wear in your sleeping bag is very much a matter of personal choice – there is no canoeists' best! The clothing you take on a tour should be easily washable and reasonably crease resistant. I have already suggested the actual canoeing outfit, and you should have a spare set of these clothes. For shopping or sightseeing a pair of terylene trousers, drip-dry shirt and a sweater will do very well. Girls swap the trousers and shirt for a skirt and blouse. If it rains wear your anorak; a pair of light shoes and a few pairs of socks and underwear complete the outfit.

When canoeing in the sun do wear a top – such as a T-shirt – for it is easy to get sunburnt very quickly and protection is less painful than the burn.

Cooking on a canoe tour demands the use of a stove. You are going to want to produce a hot meal quickly and for this a stove is essential no matter how romantic a camp fire may seem when thought of in the comfort of your home. The most common type of stove used by canoeists is the paraffin pressure stove. Several versions are available and one with a fuel capacity of one pint will prove satisfactory. The collapsible sort which takes to pieces and fits into a box is cheapest but more convenient is one which is ready to use – its metal box opens to form the pot stand. A similar stove is available which burns petrol, the only advantage being that it is possible to adjust the flame without the need to pump because the petrol vaporises in the tank and creates its own pressure.

Butane and propane gas stoves are becoming more popular and are excellent so long as you can obtain refills but this may prove difficult in some of the places a canoeist finds himself. If you intend to do a minimum of cooking it is possible to manage with a spirit stove burning solid or liquid methylated spirit. These stoves are very cheap to buy but expensive to use and it is worthwhile buying a good quality paraffin stove as soon as you can afford one.

Cooking utensils should be of aluminium for lightness and their non-rusting properties. They could initially be borrowed from the kitchen; you will need a small frying pan and a saucepan. The frying pan should be capable of acting as a lid on the saucepan. It could also double as a plate but aluminium for plates is not completely satisfactory as it soon becomes heavily scored with knife cuts; a deep enamelled plate is worth the extra weight. Camping equipment catalogues illustrate canteens of pans for camping; if you buy one of these get the sort with two saucepans and a frying pan lid with a slip-in handle. Kettles, teapots and other odd items are best left at home.

An unbreakable plastic mug is the best type and a normal knife, fork and spoon set is most convenient – some excellent stainless steel ones are available quite cheaply.

When you are cooking do not rely too much on the frying pan, it is just as easy to produce an appetising hot-pot as it is to fry sausages. Canoeists usually have a good breakfast and then a cold lunch with perhaps a hot drink or soup if the weather is bad or there has been a capsize. At the end of the day comes the main meal which should always include some meat or fish followed by fruit.

Water for cooking must be carried or obtained from a reliable source at the site. No matter how pure the river water appears to be or how desolate the country through which it flows it is always possible there is a dead sheep further upstream. A collapsible plastic water bottle of one gallon capacity is cheap and can be filled during the afternoon if you are likely to be camping away from any houses or farms. Try to buy fresh food as often as you can during a tour; do not keep meat overnight for it is liable to become contaminated and still appear satisfactory until you become ill after eating it!

Dehydrated foods are not comparable with fresh but are useful in an emergency. The soups are quite good – try the varieties before you start and take the ones you enjoy most. Tinned food is useful too but again should be looked upon as a mainly stand-by food for when you are unable to shop.

Shopping is simplified if you decide on some suitable evening meal menus before you start the trip. You will then have some idea of what you are going to buy on each shopping day. The menu need not be fixed but your original plan will be there if needed.

As with any form of camping it is advisable for the beginner to make a short trial cruise before undertaking a summer holiday tour. Have a one night camp after a short trip on your local river and iron out any snags.

The first thing you will have to learn is how to pack your canoe. To do this you will need some of the waterproof kit bags I have already described. Several small bags are easier to fit into the canoe than a few large ones. Do not overfill them, any airspace you leave will add to the buoyancy of the canoe. When you pack the canoe two aims must be borne in mind; the canoe must float on an even keel when it is loaded – this is known as 'trimming' the canoe – secondly, items which are going to be needed first on arrival must be packed last. The tent and cooking apparatus are obvious items in this category. Spare canoeing clothes may be needed quickly and should be packed in their own waterproof bag so that wet clothing can be packed away from dry. Shopping clothes may be packed with your sleeping bag. Washing equipment should also have a bag to itself; do not take one large towel, it is much better to have two small ones which will be easier to dry – in fact if you have had a baby in the family recently you will find old nappies ideal as camping towels – well washed of course! Three of these take less room than a bath towel and on a long tour are easily washed and dried.

When you pack your canoe do not have anything loose in the cockpit which can get lost or in the way if you should capsize. (Although I am constantly mentioning the possibility of capsizing it is quite normal to spend a lifetime of spare-time canoeing without ever capsizing accidentally. If you canoe on rapid rivers or the sea where a capsize is more likely your technique must be improved to take care of this, e.g. by learning to Eskimo roll and some of the methods of rescue which can be used in the sea.)

Ideally pack your canoe when it is in the water; certainly you should not try to pick it up when it is fully loaded or you will be likely to break its back. For portages which involve the use of the trolley it is safe to leave some kit in the end which is supported by the trolley – you will have to carry the remainder. A frameless rucksack is useful for this and when it is in the canoe it can be used to hold together those items which do not have to be in completely water-proof bags, e.g. tinned food. A framed rucksack is useless in a canoe.

For a short portage where two of you are carrying the canoe the kit may be left in the ends, but *not* in the middle. Camping techniques are well covered in many specialised books but there are a few points peculiar to the canoeist who is a camper from necessity.

Follow the standard procedure of all mobile campers and seek permission before pitching your tent. Enquire at the nearest house when you find a suitable site; if the house owner does not own the site you have chosen he will often be able to tell you who does. The only exception to this is if there is no house in sight or if you are going to camp on a tow path. This is not recommended. The path which was deserted when you arrived in the late afternoon will be full of evening strollers later, all eager to trip over your guy lines. For this reason avoid camping too near any group of houses.

Islands are sometimes possible camp sites but they are often very overgrown and mosquitoes, always a problem near the river, may prove excessively lively! As you will be staying only overnight there is no need to be too fussy but do remember that rivers in hilly country are likely to flood their banks if it rains heavily during the night. This is not a problem in lowland areas for the surrounding fields absorb the water and release it into the river more slowly. Avoid fields where cattle are grazing for they are extremely inquisitive and will insist on standing around the tent all night breathing heavily.

Once the tent is erected get your sleeping bag out to air and set up your stove in the lee of the tent. Do not cook in the tent unless it is absolutely necessary – the fire risk is very great and the tent is liable to be damaged by fat or greasy steam. In all but the heaviest rain a hedge or tree will provide ample shelter for the stove.

For washing it is normal to use the river water unless this is obviously badly contaminated, as it may be below a large town. Washing up is most easily done in very hot water with a little detergent added. Use your largest pan and wash the non-greasy items first. Do not use a canvas bowl for washing up for it soon becomes saturated with dirty grease and is impossible to clean. For this reason dispose of your dirty water well under a hedge where it will cause no bother to anyone wishing to camp after you.

Sanitation is always something of a problem for the mobile camper and here again the aim is to avoid any chance of causing offence to anyone. A small trowel can be carried together with a supply of toilet paper – keep this dry!

Suggested list of camping equipment

Items marked with an asterisk could be shared
* Tent including accessories such as groundsheet and flysheet
  Sleeping bag and lining
* Cooking stove
* Cooking utensils
  Plate, mug and cutlery
* Sharp knife for cutting bread

* Candles and matches in waterproof container
* Dish cloth and drying cloth
* Tin opener
  Personal toilet items
* Toilet paper and small trowel
* First aid kit
* Torch
* Drinking water bottles
  Waterproof bags, frameless rucksacks
* String shopping bag
  Sunglasses
  Insect repellent
* Canoe repair kit
  Personal clothing
* Canvas bowl
* Spare fuel and canvas windshield for the stove

This is not intended as an exhaustive list. Other items will occur to you but, as with any other form of mobile camping, do not burden yourself with something you are going to use once during the tour – try doing without it.

8 Canoeing for groups

So far I have been considering the individual who wants to begin canoeing; there are also a considerable number of groups of various types for whom canoeing is a practicable and enjoyable sport. What has already been written will be applicable to the group no less than the individual but there there are also additional points of particular interest to them.

The first consideration is the type of canoe to be made or bought. Single-seat canoes are probably the most generally useful but have the disadvantage that they cost hardly any less than the two-seater. Here then is an economy measure for a group – make mostly two-seat canoes. I write 'mostly' for when the individual members of the group get their own canoes they should be encouraged to obtain singles; two or three group singles, preferably of differing designs, will whet their appetites accordingly.

This raises the question of design and form of construction. Since the group will be requiring several canoes a method of construction involving the use of a mould or jig may be an economic proposition although not necessary if a *DK* design is used. Fibre-glass construction is rather ambitious unless you are experienced in canoe building generally and you would be well advised to build with plywood.

Multiple production of the *DK* designs is straightforward. If a powered jig-saw is available it is easy to cut out several hull panels at once by pinning or stapling the sheets of plywood together and marking out the top sheet. You will then be able to work on several canoes in sequence. The only limit to this is the working space and manpower available.

It is also possible to buy plans or kits for various other types of plywood canoe and addresses may be obtained from

Plate 28 A two seat touring canoe.

the magazines listed in the last chapter. Kits will cost about twice as much as building from scratch and a ready-made canoe, of the same type, some three times as much. I discount fibre-glass canoes here for they are not as yet much built by amateurs.

The group might also try to obtain one or two racing craft, perhaps a *K1* and a *K2*. Club boats are often the only way a beginner can start competitive canoeing for the canoes are very expensive although prices may become lower as more British makers enter the market. The Canadian canoe should also be considered for one of these will enable three or four young paddlers to go afloat and learn the art of handling a single-bladed paddle. There are a few fibre-glass Canadian types available at present and one multi-chine plywood and glass tape design which is also available as a kit.

86

Once the group has started its canoeing activities all members should be encouraged to join the BCU and the group can become affiliated. Membership is essential if members of the group intend to make up competitive canoeing. Help can be obtained with coaching and the passing of the BCU Proficiency Test could be made a condition of being allowed to take part in group tours. There is of course nothing to prevent the group having their own series of tests leading up to the Proficiency Test. The Boys' Brigade have introduced a canoeing badge with their own tests and the Duke of Edinburgh's Award Scheme has three proficiency standards which are closely allied to the BCU tests. Canoeing is only part of the Scheme which offers to boys and girls of between fourteen and twenty years a 'challenge to endeavour and achievement through a balanced programme of leisure time activities.'

Canoeing with the group is little different to solo canoeing – you still paddle your own canoe! It is necessary to take up a definite form when paddling in a party. There must be an experienced leader and another experienced member following the party to keep watch on the slower members and to help with any repairs. It is normal procedure to have one competent canoeist to about six beginners; thus a large party might be in two or more smaller groups. These smaller groups should never be less than three including one competent canoeist. At all times members of each group should remain in visual contact.

Some pre-arranged silent signals should be learnt so the leader can control the party without a lot of disturbing noise, e.g. a right hand raised might mean come together at the right bank. It may be necessary to use whistle signals when it would be impractical to stop paddling, e.g. on a rapid river or the sea. Signals would be of use if the party meets a fisherman on a popular fishing river. The party should stop some way from the fisherman while the leader asks permission for the party to pass. If this is granted pass quickly but with as little disturbance as possible and no noise. Politeness of this kind costs nothing and may prove helpful to future canoeists. If permission to canoe past is withheld there is nothing for it but to portage – again as quietly as possible and without fuss.

For a small party – perhaps three or four canoes – camping can take the same form as that for the solo or pair of canoeists. A larger party, however, should make prior arrangements for sites and sanitary facilities must be more elaborate. With a party involving perhaps twenty or more members the fixed camp may be the best answer. Transport is always the problem with this scheme and for a large number of people a coach plus transport for the canoes may be necessary. If the transport problem can be surmounted the camp is set up at a convenient point about half way along the section of river to be canoed and the canoeing party is taken to the starting place each day by the transport. For a week of canoeing an outward journey of perhaps thirty miles would be involved on the first and last days.

In this kind of camp a large tent with an extended flysheet is useful as a kitchen and dining tent. The scheme can be modified by having more than one camp site so less road travelling is involved.

A similar scheme is sometimes used for tours on rapid rivers when a vehicle is used to transport camping equipment from site to site and the canoeists carry only lunch and personal items which may be required during the day. This works very well if there is a member of the party who is not keen on canoeing but would enjoy exploring the countryside during the day. Parents can sometimes be persuaded to do this.

The activities of the group need not be confined to cruises; competitive canoeing can be arranged and although national long distance races are over a distance of ten miles or more a short race of a mile or so will be popular and well within the capabilities of relative beginners. A race of this kind has been organised in Canterbury for the past two years and may well become an annual 'round the town' event.

Many events of a non-serious nature can be devised such as canoe polo, played with an inflated ball; backwards races; hand paddling races; timed rescue competition and wiggle and wriggle tests. These latter are a kind of miniature slalom course which can be fitted into a small river or even a swimming pool. A course card is obtainable from the BCU.

Finally, and on a more serious note, the leader of any group should ascertain the extent of his responsibility and arrange appropriate insurance cover.

9 A guide to canoe competition

While this book is primarily concerned with canoeing as a recreation it is impossible to consider a sport without its competitive aspects. Most canoeists do at some time indulge in one or more of the competitive forms of canoeing; if only their local long distance race once a year or the club slalom. Certainly competition plays a large part in the lives of many canoeists and to be fair to you, the reader, who may be a budding world champion slalomist, I am including this chapter to give a short account of the canoeing competition currently available in this country.

The most popular form of competition at present is *long distance* racing. LD races may be on sea, river or canal or a combination of all three; they are usually over ten miles long with shortened courses for ladies and juniors. The great advantage of LD racing is that a very specialised canoe is not necessary; the races are organised in four classes each with an open, junior and ladies division.

Class one is for international single *K1*s, about 17 feet long with a beam of 20 inches; class two for international double *K2*s, about $21\frac{1}{2}$ feet long with a beam of 22 inches; class three for touring singles with a maximum length of 15 feet and a minimum beam of 23 inches and class four for touring doubles with a maximum length of 18 feet and a minimum waterline beam of 21 inches with a gunwale beam of 24 inches. Special LD craft have been developed for these two classes but it is still possible to race a normal touring canoe if it is within the class rules.

The successful LD paddler has to train seriously and must include winter training in his schedule. As in other forms of canoe competition considerable travelling is involved to reach race sites in different parts of the country.

Sprint racing takes place on flat water with no problems as to portageing or natural hazards which may face the LD racer. There are five sprint classes, *K1* singles, *K2* doubles, *K4*s with a crew of four, *C1* Canadian singles and *C2* Canadian doubles. Races are held over distances of 500, 1,000 and 10,000 metres.

The canoeist who aspires to sprint racing has first to learn to balance the very specialised canoe he is to use. Membership of a club is essential and a strict training programme must be drawn up and adhered to. The ultimate reward in sprint racing is selection to represent Great Britain in the Olympic Games.

Slalom is another popular branch of canoe sport but here again the canoes used have become more specialised and to reach the top divisions a first class boat is required. The canoes conform to international rules as to size; *K1*s have a minimum length of 4 metres and beam of 60 centimetres; the *C1* has the same minimum length but a beam of 80 centimetres; the *C2* has a minimum length of 4·58 metres

Plate 29 At the start of an LD race.

with a beam of 80 centimetres. All slalom canoes have well-rockered keels to aid turning and the *K* class boats have low ends to minimise the chances of hitting the gate poles. The cross-sectional shape of the hull is elliptical to reduce water resistance and facilitate rolling in the event of a capsize. Cockpit size is kept small and even the Canadian classes have only a round cockpit in which the paddler kneels – their decking and slightly upturned ends give them a distinctive banana shape.

The object of the slalom is to provide a course which tests the canoeists' skill in rough water; the competitor is timed over the course and the better of two attempts is counted. Eskimo rolling is allowed during a run but a capsize without a roll means disqualification for that attempt. Slalomists have to wear an approved life-jacket and may be required to wear a crash helmet.

Beginners start in the novice events and after competing in two such events during one season they are promoted to division three; further promotion to divisions two and one are on results. Ladies have their own divisions and are promoted when their score in a particular slalom is within 10 per cent of the winning man's score.

White water racing is simply a straightforward race against the clock over a given length of rapid river. To enter one of these races it is necessary to achieve a certain standard of proficiency in rapid river canoeing, e.g. by being a first or second division slalomist.

Slalom boats may be used but again more specialised craft are now available and a maximum length rule is applied of 4·5 metres for the *K1*, 4·3 metres for the *C1* and 5·0 metres for the *C2*. A white water ranking list is compiled from the results of a series of ranking races held during the winter months.

With the exception of sprint racing canoes most racing craft are now made from glass-fibre reinforced plastics – almost essential to withstand the wear of slalom and white water work. This is not to say that you cannot compete in other types of canoe providing they conform to the rules concerned,

92

but with the various craft becoming more specialised every year very good results cannot be expected.

If you feel drawn to one of the forms of competition join a club which takes an interest in this aspect and find out all you can before committing yourself to a class boat. You will probably be able to borrow a boat to try and if you are keen will be given every encouragement.

10 A start in sea canoeing

Sea canoeing is perhaps the most hazardous form of canoeing since it is impossible to anticipate with certainty the moods of the sea. The canoeist must reduce the dangers by taking every precaution and safeguard.

To take a canoe to sea in its proper sense, where you may be out of sight of land for many hours or even days, requires a knowledge of seamanship which is beyond the scope of this book to impart. Certainly this is not for the beginner in a canoe.

My aim here is to explain the requirements of sea canoeing and encourage you to seek further information and advice if this kind of canoeing appeals to you. Your equipment is most important, for here more than elsewhere in canoeing your life will depend on its suitability for the job you are expecting it to do.

Your canoe should be in perfect condition and preferably fitted with a rudder which makes it easier to maintain your course when you are being battered by wind and waves. The best type of canoe for the experienced is one of the modern versions of the Greenland Eskimo kayak; this is for the expert or the beginner under expert supervision. A canoe which is good on the sea has a long, straight keel line and rounded sections with some flare toward the gunwales. The cockpit should be small and the spray cover a really good fit.

Buoyancy must be fixed into position at both ends. One or two painters are essential as they may provide the only means of rescuing the canoe if you capsize and your single-seat canoe may weigh nearly 1,000 lbs when it is full of water! Paddles must be sound and a spare should be carried – this will have to be a two-piece type and can be held to the deck by means of elastic cords.

A reliable compass must be carried together with an up-to-date chart of the area. The chart can be sealed into a waterproof cover otherwise it will rapidly disintegrate into a sodden mass. These two items may seem unduly pessimistic if you intend to paddle along the coast only a few hundred yards offshore. They are one of our safeguards. A sea fog can arrive more quickly than you can paddle – especially if you have an adverse tide. Nothing will make you more lonely than a fog at sea when you can see the bow of your canoe and nothing else. Imagine yourself in this position and you will appreciate the need for a chart and compass. You may even be swept out to sea if you cannot reach your destination before the tide turns against you – an unlikely happening if your preparation has been well done, but it is possible.

The charts published for yachtsmen are easy to use and smaller than the Admiralty ones.

A packet of suitable flares should be carried where they can be reached even in a rough sea or if you are capsized – this is when you are likely to need them most. A good place would be in a pocket on the front of the spray cover; avoid a zip fastener for this pocket, use the nylon 'touch' fastening which is easily pulled open.

You will of course be wearing your life-jacket which ought to have a plastic whistle and a lifting becket attached. At sea it is almost impossible to remain dry, all you can hope to do is keep warm. The easiest way to achieve this is to wear a 'wet suit'; this is closely-fitting suit of thin sponge rubber which traps a layer of water next to your skin and insulates it from outside conditions. The layer of water quickly reaches body temperature and thereafter you will remain warm. If you buy a wet suit – and they can be made – do make sure you get one recommended for canoeing which is a good fit. Looseness can set up chafe which will result in soreness and consequent lack of efficiency – a dangerous situation at sea.

Closely allied to warmth is comfort. Make sure your seat is comfortable before you set out, for once you are at sea it will be too late to alter it. With warmth and comfort care and efficiency are easily maintained; cold and discomfort will make you dispirited and liable to make mistakes.

The most important safeguard once you have all your equipment assembled is preparation. Find out all you can about the area you are going to canoe. Study the chart and learn the easily recognised landmarks – remember you are going to be only a couple of feet above sea-level! Pick out the beaches suitable for landing and those which are not. Buy a copy of the local tide tables and work your route so you will be helped by the tide. Before you set out inform the coast guard of your intentions and take his advice as to the conditions. *If you have any doubts do not go.*

No sea-canoeing expedition should have less than three canoes taking part. It is possible for two canoeists to perform a deep water rescue if the third capsizes and is unable to roll himself upright. This type of rescue must be practised before the expedition until it can be successfully completed in any conditions.

Launching and landing can be quite a problem especially from a surf beach. Always remember that the waves are far stronger than you and if you allow your canoe to become swamped it will be difficult to rescue without damage being caused. Usually the best system involves getting into the canoe between waves and getting off the beach before fitting the spray cover; any water which finds its way inside can be sponged out when the calmer water is reached offshore. Landing can sometimes be affected in a similar way; or let the canoe swing broadside to the waves and step out on the seaward side in shallow water – on the seaward side to avoid being knocked from your feet by the canoe.

Camping on a sea tour can also present problems especially if the beach is shingle. Whenever possible try to pitch the tent on grass – sand makes a disastrous camping companion quite apart from the difficulty of making the tent stay up. This may mean carrying the canoes and kit some yards from the beach and the recommended order here is for one member of the party to pitch the tent or tents first while the canoes and remaining gear are brought to the site. Once the tents are erected the stoves can be lighted and the evening meal started.

96

If you plan to enter a river or harbour arrange to travel on the flooding tide otherwise entry may prove impossible. Care must be taken too if there is a 'bar' at the mouth where the tide meets the outflowing river. Many rivers, particularly on the east coast, have wide areas of mud exposed at low tide; again try to arrange your travelling so you reach your destination when the tide is covering the mud. Considerable planning may be needed but this is half the fun of sea canoeing and on grounds of safety alone should not be skimped.

When your sea cruise is over and you are back on your familiar river do some practice capsizes and give the canoe a good wash with fresh water to remove the salt. A fresh water wash is most important if you have any brass or aluminium fittings as these will corrode if sea water is allowed to act upon them.

11 Maintenance and repairs

If you have already built your own canoe maintenance will present no difficulties. Maintenance is not necessarily an annual affair. Canoes by their very nature tend to be well used and you should get into the habit of inspecting your canoe at the end of every trip or at the end of each day of a particularly rough water cruise. For normal, permanent, repair work the canoe must be completely dry; glue, paint and varnish just do not work on wet canoes.

Normal maintenance will involve repainting or varnishing as necessary together with the replacement or repair of accessories. Check buoyancy, spray cover and painters.

If your canoe is single-skin plywood, like the *DK* designs, an excellent permanent repair can be made with a fibre-glass patch. When this type of hardskin canoe is holed the plywood can be pushed back into place and the patch put on the inside if it is accessible. With the patch on the inside allow the resin to run into the damaged wood and file off the excess when it has cured. Any remaining small holes or roughness can be filled from the outside using resin mixed with chopped fibre-glass.

An outside patch is simple and should be made as neatly as possible then glasspapered smooth when cured. Before applying the patch it is essential to remove all traces of varnish or paint in the area to be covered. The usual polyester resin will not adhere to wet or damp materials so for a temporary repair to a plywood or fibre-glass canoe it is necessary to use a soft sealing compound, such as Seelastik, covered on the outside with adhesive tape. I have used plastic-based electrical tape which sticks to a surface which has been well wiped so as to be clean and reasonably dry. This method is only of use on a small hole or fracture in the

98

skin. More extensive temporary repairs can be made by 'stitching' a plywood patch in place with short lengths of copper wire or nailing with small copper or brass nails which are clenched over on the inside. Normal nailing or screwing is useless as the plywood is too thin and flexible for holding to be satisfactory. The patch should be coated liberally with sealing compound before fixing into place. This makes an unsightly but practical repair.

A permanent repair to a sizeable hole in a plywood or moulded veneer hull is made by first cutting the hole to a regular shape. A piece of plywood, larger than the hole, is pinned and glued inside the hull and then a patch the exact size of the hole is glued in place. If the patch is to be on a sharply curved section of the hull it will be necessary to fasten a larger piece of plywood over the outside to hold the patch in place while the glue is setting.

A similar procedure is followed when repairing a fibre-glass hull. The edges of the hole are first frayed to enable the resin to bond well to the hull; then a piece of stiff card, its inside face covered with polythene to prevent sticking, is taped over the outside of the hole. A piece of chopped mat is cut to fit the hole with a little overlap onto the hull. The mat is then coated with resin and well stippled into place; this is repeated until the patch is the same thickness as the canoe skin. If it is available the first coat of resin should be gel coat coloured to match the hull colour. When the patch is cured the card is removed.

To make this repair inside access is necessary; if the hole is inaccessible from the cockpit the patch must be applied from the outside.

Soft skin repairs are simply a matter of sticking on a patch using the appropriate adhesive for the skin material. If the damage is extensive the material must be drawn together with thread first using a herring bone stitch.

Framework damage is usually repairable with copper wire and a short length of stringer or a piece of plywood. Your emergency repair kit should include the following items well wrapped in a waterproof bag and securely fastened in an accessible place in your canoe.

For the hard skin canoe

Pliers
Bradawl
Sharp knife
Copper wire
Some small brass screws and screwdriver to fit
$\frac{3}{4}$-inch brass or copper nails
Sealing compound
Adhesive plastic tape
Small tin of waterproof glue
A few offcuts of waterproof 3-mm plywood

For the soft skin canoe

All the above plus hull material offcuts and suitable cement, needle and thread, scissors and a length of stringer section which could be taped to a stringer or floorboard.

Most of the expendable items could be bought *en route* if further stocks are required. As already mentioned only one repair kit is needed for each two or three canoes and the last member of the party must carry it in his canoe.

12 Useful information

In this chapter I have collected together some of the odds and ends of information which the beginner to canoeing is likely to find useful.

Knots

As a canoeist you will need to know how to tie a few knots; the six illustrated overleaf will between them serve you quite adequately.

(a) Figure-of-eight knot usually tied in the end of a rope to prevent it pulling through an eyelet or block.
(b) Reef knot used for joining two ropes of equal thickness.
(c) Clove hitch useful for tying up to a post or tree; it will withstand a pull along the post.
(d) Round turn and two half hitches, also used for tying to a post or ring.
(e) Sheet bend for joining ropes of unequal thickness or tying to an eyelet or ring. Can be made 'quick release' by pushing a loop (bight) through instead of the end.
(f) Bowline makes a non-slip loop, a most useful knot.

The BCU inland proficiency test for kayaks – decked canoes

Passing this test would mean that you could be considered reasonably safe under normal water conditions. The test has to be taken on water flowing at about 3 m.p.h.

1. Candidates must demonstrate the following knots and show that they know the functions of them: reef knot, sheet bend, bowline, figure-of-eight, round turn and two half hitches.
2. The candidate will present his kayak and the following items for inspection when they are ready for use: paddle, bow and stern lines, buoyancy, life-jacket, repair kit. It is also

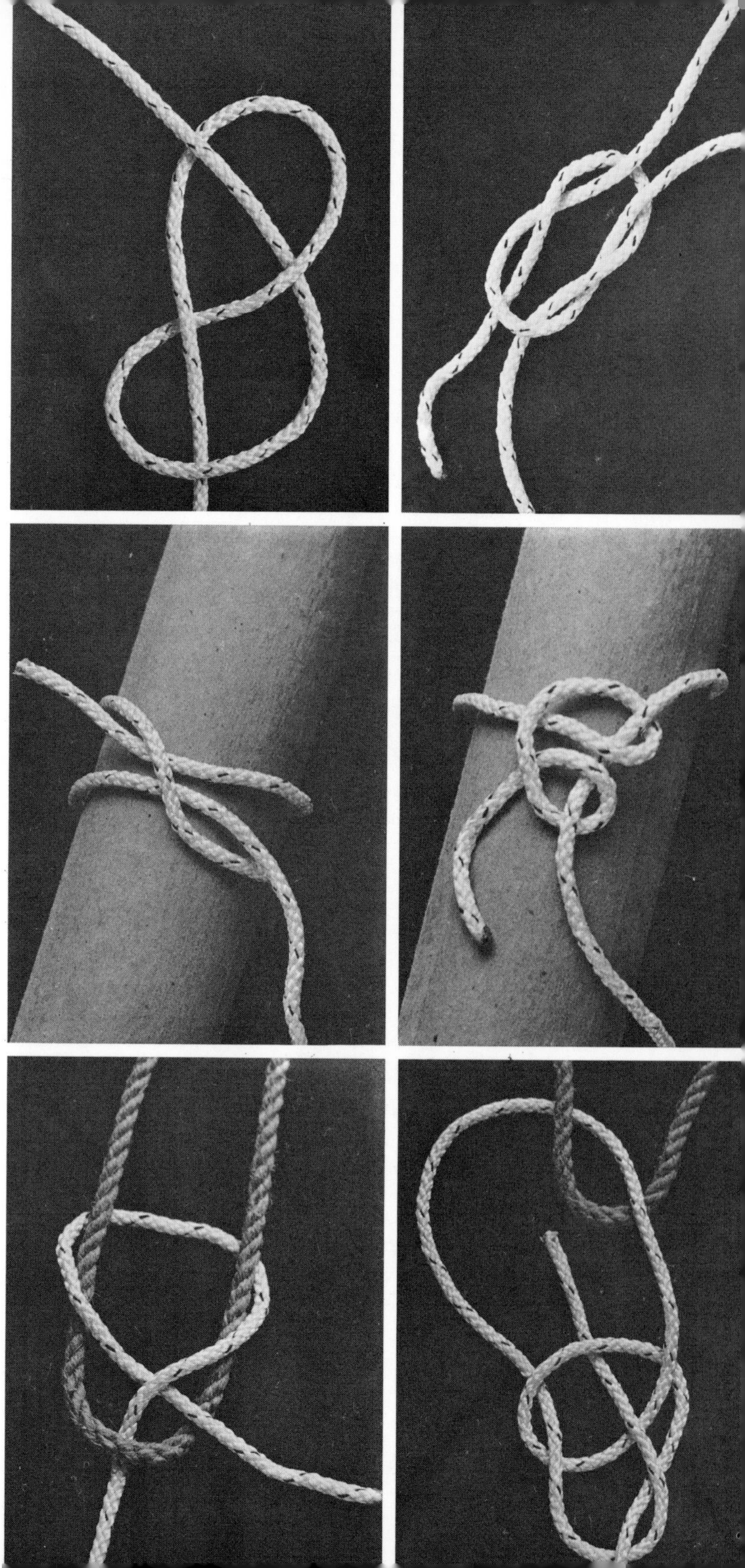

Plate 30 Six knots
Figure of eight
knot.
Reef knot.
Clove hitch.
Round turn and
two half-hitches.
Sheet bend.
Bowline.

strongly recommended that spray covers be provided.

3. The candidate will pack his kayak as if in preparation for a journey of two or three days.

4. The candidate will handle his kayak into the water. The canoe will be made fast to the bank and left.

5. The candidate will get into his kayak from the bank and will then put out into midstream.

6. The candidate will be required to paddle his kayak upstream in an efficient manner for about fifty yards. He will then turn and paddle back to his starting point. He will demonstrate emergency stopping in both directions, and coming alongside.

7. He will demonstrate the following strokes: sweep (forward and reverse), draw, slap support, support sculling, sculling draw.

8. He will show that he understands the principles of the ferry glide, facing down and upstream.

9. He will capsize his loaded kayak in midstream, bring it back to the bank and empty out the water.

10. He will re-embark standing in water at knee depth. He will then return to the bank, disembark, take the kayak from the water and place it properly on the bank.

11. The candidate will swim 50 yards in light clothing, e.g. shirt, shorts, gym shoes, without a life-jacket. He will then swim 25 yards wearing a fully inflated life-jacket.

12. Candidates should be prepared to answer general questions on safety put to them by the examiner.

13. Candidates should be aware of the access problem with regard to canoeing in their own locality and show a knowledge of the BCU River Advisory Service.

For items 4, 9 and 10 the candidate may have assistance if he so desires. Throughout 'he' may also be read as 'she'! Further tests are available for Canadian canoes; sea and open water in the kayak and advanced tests.

The international system of grading rivers

1. Easy. Rivers with this grading may have small rapids, care will be needed where the river is narrow and obstacles such as shallows may occur.

2. Medium. Frequent rapids with regular waves and small

eddies and whirlpools. The best course is usually easy to find.
3. Difficult. Numerous rapids with broken water, high irregular waves, whirlpools and eddies. The best course is not easy to find.
4. Very difficult. Inspection should be made from the bank before attempting this grade of rapid.
5. Exceedingly difficult. Inspection essential. Rapids will have long, unbroken stretches with very fast eddies, submerged rocks and difficult whirlpools.
6. The absolute limit of difficulty. Cannot be attempted without risk to life.

Beginners should not attempt anything beyond grade 3 and this only with an experienced leader. The grading is given for the normal water conditions; abnormal conditions may change the grading. In most cases the grading given in a waterway guide is only an average for the river. Two numbers may be used where necessary.

National clubs

The British Canoe Union, 26/29 Park Crescent, London W1, controls all canoe competition in Britain and can supply information on canoeing including specialist advice on the use of certain rivers by River Advisors. The Union also maintains a stock of books and maps of interest to canoeists and publishes booklets on various aspects of canoeing.

The Canoe Camping Club, 11 Lower Grosvenor Place, London SW1, is a section of the Camping Club of Great Britain and Ireland and has regional groups throughout Britain. The club offers all the facilities of the Camping Club as well as many canoeist orientated services.

Magazines

Canoeing Magazine, Canoeing Press, 25 Featherbed Lane, Croydon, Surrey, CRO 9AE. Monthly by subscription, 21s per year.

Canoeing in Britain, published by the BCU for members. Quarterly.

White Water, 21 Windsor Road, Manchester 10. Quarterly by subscription, 10s per year.

The Canoe Camper, published by the CCC for members. Quarterly.

Camping and Outdoor Life, published by the Camping Club. Monthly, supplied to members of the CCC.

Light Craft. Monthly from bookstalls; has canoeing reports and articles of interest to canoeists.

Books

Guide to the Waterways of the British Isles (BCU, 21s).
Canoeing Waters, Percy W. Blandford (Lutterworth Press, 18s 6d).
Coastwise Navigation, G. G. Watkins (Kandy Publications, 5s).
A Thousand Miles in the Rob Roy Canoe, J. MacGregor (BCU reprints, 10s 6d).
Canoeing (American Red Cross – available from the BCU, 15s). A most authoritative work on Canadian canoeing.
Canoeing, William Bliss (out of print, should be available through your public library).
Wiggle Test Cards (from BCU, 2s 6d per dozen).

Additional books: which should be available from your public library:

Kingfisher Abroad – T. & T. Rising
Canoe Errant – Major R. Raven-Hart
both on pre-war touring in Europe.
Under Sail Through Red Devon – R. B. Cattell
river and coastal canoeing in Devon.
Canoeing Down the Rhone – John Wilson
to the Mediterranean in the 1950's.
Quest by Canoe – A. M. Dunnett
Glasgow to Skye by canoe.
Rapid Rivers – William Bliss
Canadian canoeing in England.

Equipment

Up-to-date addresses of those firms supplying materials, canoes and kits may be obtained from current copies of the magazines.

The Water Sports Code

This is a booklet of recommendations for the users of inland waterways. Copies may be obtained from the Central

Council of Physical Recreation, 26 Park Crescent, London W1. However, the specific suggestions for canoeists are:

1. Keep away from banks where anglers are fishing.
2. Keep well clear of anglers' tackle, do not loiter in fishing pools, and cause as little disturbance as possible.
3. Keep a sharp lookout for fishermen. Comply with any signals they make to indicate whether they wish you to wait for a moment or pass. Give a hail if you think your approach has been unnoticed.
4. Be particularly careful not to touch anglers' lines.
5. Do not alter course so as to baulk other craft, particularly in narrow waters. Remember that larger boats are less easily manoeuvrable, and that canoes can use much shallower water than other craft.
6. Keep clear of rowing craft – sculls, fours and eights – particularly when racing or serious coaching is taking place. Remember that it is sometimes difficult for rowing craft to see canoes.

DK construction

If you should require any further information regarding the construction of the *DK 12* or details of other *DK* designs the author will be pleased to assist you on receipt of a stamped addressed envelope. Enquiries of this type may be sent to:

> Dennis J. Davis
> *The Book of Canoeing*
> c/o Arthur Barker Ltd
> 5 Winsley Street
> London W1

Some Safety Rules

Don't canoe if you cannot swim.

Do provide buoyancy for your canoe and a life-jacket for yourself where a capsize would be dangerous – in the sea, heavy rapids, floods and cold water.

Do ask about local conditions: tides, currents, rapids and weather changes can all be dangerous.

Don't go out alone without having told someone where you are going and how long you are going to be.

Don't put more people into a canoe than it is designed to carry.

Don't wear wellingtons – you cannot swim in heavy boots.

Don't change places while afloat.

Do keep clear of other craft.

Do keep away from weirs – they are often dangerous.

Don't right a capsized canoe – hang on to it. It will float and you may not.

Don't be put off by this list – it is all common-sense really.

Do remember – better safe than sorry.

Glossary

Anorak – waterproof jacket, usually fitted with a hood.

Beam – maximum width of a boat.

Bight – a loop in a rope.

Bow – front of a boat.

Broken water – water breaking on rocks.

Chine – the angle between the bottom and side of a hard chine or multi chine hull.

Coaming – external rim of the cockpit.

Eddy – slack water moving against the stream when the main flow passes a bay. The current is fastest at the outside. Usually a good place to land on rapid rivers.

Eskimo roll – a complete roll, capsizing one side and up on the other.

Glass-fibre – glass in the form of a filament which may be woven into cloth or tape.

Gunwale – the top edge of a hull.

Keel – the central, external lengthwise member of a hull.

Keelson (hog) – the internal member of the hull above the keel.

Lining down – allowing the empty canoe to float down a rapid or shallow stretch controlled by the painters.

Lock – a means of raising or lowering a boat from one level of a river or canal to another.

Painter – a strong, light line attached to the ends of a canoe for mooring and other purposes.

Plywood – an odd number of thin sheets of wood glued together with the grain at right angles.

Pound – a section of canal between locks.

Rapid – an increase in the speed of the current resulting in waves.

Scarf joint – a method of joining wood or plywood without

increasing the thickness.

Sluices (slackers) – used to empty or fill a lock.

Spanish windlass – a method of cramping by twisting a piece of wood or a similar lever in a loop of rope.

Stern – back of a boat.

Stopper – a large wave, often below a weir.

Thwart – transverse member in a Canadian canoe.

Weir – a wall to retain a head of water in the upper level of a river. Water flows over it.

Whirlpool – water turning on a definite axis. Fastest at the centre; the opposite of 'eddy'.

Index